More Praise for *Breaking the Trust Barrier*

"As a leader in situations that are literally life-or-death, JV brings street cred to the challenge of leading high-performance teams. His examples come from the physics of close-formation aerial maneuvers and the incredibly small tolerances that make the difference between good and extraordinary. With quiet humor and humility, he uses those stories to offer insight and actionable advice leader to leader."
—**Mark E. White, Principal, Global Consulting Chief Technology Officer, Deloitte Consulting, LLP**

"JV does an amazing job of sharing powerful real-life examples that we can implement in our organizations. A fascinating read that delivers a message so powerful yet practical. This book should be required reading for all leaders looking to take their teams to new heights!"
—**Bob Korzeniewski, Executive Vice President for Strategic Development, Verisign Inc., 2000-2007**

"Even though this was written by the 'competition,' I found *Breaking the Trust Barrier* to be a great read. JV delivers a powerful message in a way that will stay with you and your team for years to come. Drafting is not just a process for building and leading high-performance teams; it's a pathway to success."
—**Rob "Ice" Ffield, Blue Angels Flight Leader/Commanding Officer, 2001–2002, and President and CEO, CATSHOT Group, LLC**

"*Breaking the Trust Barrier* is a leader's must-read! JV masterfully combines his Air Force experiences with thoughtful insights from commanding the world-famous Thunderbirds to create a road map for building real trust. He talks so honestly about commitment, loyalty, and trust that his message easily translates to any business or leadership environment. I honestly can't wait to apply much of what I have read with my own team."
—**Dennis M. Satyshur, Director of Golf Operations, Caves Valley Golf Club**

"JV clearly articulates the key to his success leading multiple organizations and gives readers a glimpse of the challenge, excitement, and emotion of leading a high-performance jet demonstration team. I followed JV in ⟨ ⟩ on the principle ⟨ ⟩ ok inspiring, pr⟨ ⟩ author⟨ ⟩"
—**Richard "**⟨ ⟩ ⟨ ⟩ls,
2002-200⟨ ⟩ rier : ⟨ ⟩ ⟨ ⟩aps fo⟨ ⟩

"Multiple commands and his stint as the lead pilot of the USAF Thunderbirds have given Colonel JV Venable powerful insights that he has captured in *Breaking the Trust Barrier*. His imagery will sear the themes of this book in your memory. His conception of trust is striking, memorable, and entirely new to the literature of leadership."

—Dr. Charles Ping, President Emeritus, Ohio University

"Captivating stories within *Breaking the Trust Barrier* make the process you'll find inside absolutely indelible. This is an inspiring book and, if you're like me, you'll start putting JV's techniques to work the moment you set it down. Whether you're a senior executive or just getting your footing as a leader, this is a must-read!"

—Linda Chambliss, Vice President, Global Account Operations, STARTEK

*Breaking the
Trust Barrier*

Breaking the Trust Barrier

How Leaders Close the Gaps for High Performance

JV Venable

BK

Berrett–Koehler Publishers, Inc.
a BK Business book

Berrett-Koehler Publishers, Inc.
1333 Broadway, Suite 1000, Oakland, CA 94612-1921
Tel: (510) 817-2277   Fax: (510) 817-2278   www.bkconnection.com

Ordering Information

Quantity sales. Special discounts are available on quantity purchases by corporations, associations, and others. For details, contact the "Special Sales Department" at the Berrett-Koehler address above.

Individual sales. Berrett-Koehler publications are available through most bookstores. They can also be ordered directly from Berrett-Koehler:

Tel: (800) 929-2929; Fax: (802) 864-7626; www.bkconnection.com.

Orders for college textbook/course adoption use. Please contact Berrett-Koehler:

Tel: (800) 929-2929; Fax: (802) 864-7626.

Orders by U.S. trade bookstores and wholesalers. Please contact Ingram Publisher Services, Tel: (800) 509-4887; Fax: (800) 838-1149; E-mail: customer .service@ingrampublisherservices.com; or visit www.ingrampublisherservices .com/Ordering for details about electronic ordering.

Berrett-Koehler and the BK logo are registered trademarks of Berrett-Koehler Publishers, Inc.

Printed in the United States of America

Berrett-Koehler books are printed on long-lasting acid-free paper. When it is available, we choose paper that has been manufactured by environmentally responsible processes. These may include using trees grown in sustainable forests, incorporating recycled paper, minimizing chlorine in bleaching, or recycling the energy produced at the paper mill.

Library of Congress Cataloging-in-Publication Data
Names: Venable, JV (John V.), author.
Title: Breaking the trust barrier : how leaders close the gaps for high performance / JV Venable.
Description: Oakland : Berrett-Koehler Publishers, [2016] | Includes index.
Identifiers: LCCN 2016001425 | ISBN 9781626566101 (pbk.)
Subjects: LCSH: Leadership. | Trust. | Organizational effectiveness. | Performance.
Classification: LCC HD57.7 .V46 2016 | DDC 658.4/092—dc23
LC record available at http://lccn.loc.gov/2016001425

20   19   18   17   16   10   9   8   7   6   5   4   3   2   1

Cover design by Dan Tesser; cover and title page photo by Staff Sergeant Kristi Machayo, USAF Thunderbirds. Interior design, illustration, and composition by Gary Palmatier, Ideas to Images. Elizabeth von Radics, copyeditor; Mike Mollett, proofreader; Rachel Rice, indexer.

*This book is dedicated to the men and women
of the US Air Force Thunderbirds of 2000 and 2001.*

*You served as an inspiration to millions
of Americans during our time on the team,
and you still do that for me today.*

Contents

Foreword: Can Born Leaders Teach Others to Lead?

Robert L. Jolles

Bestselling author of
Customer Centered Selling

JV Venable is a born leader. You'd sense it if you ever stood near him. You'd know it if you ever heard him speak. You'd feel it if you ever shook his hand. His backstory is inspiring, and his accomplishments are amazing, but can a born leader like JV teach *you* to lead others?

Many leaders have been dogged by this same question. After all, if these skills are so innate, can they be consciously laid out in a process for others to learn and apply? Typi-cally, those who are blessed with natural skills struggle to teach others the skills they so effortlessly command. This is because the skills that come so naturally are ones they have never really had to stop and assess.

If someone put a golf club in your hand and you could easily hit the ball 300 yards down the middle of the fairway, would you stop and study that swing? You might simply enjoy the gift you were born with. Now imagine that this same person decided to try to teach others how to duplicate that swing. It's no coincidence that those who are born with certain gifts—academic or physical—typically make poor teachers.

Ironically, it's far more common to find that the most effective teachers and coaches are not born with the skills they teach. Those skills did not come naturally to them. As a matter of fact, they learned those skills the hard way—by trial and error, bit by bit. Being consciously aware of every move you make allows you to naturally verbalize those lessons to others.

Every now and then, however, someone comes along who is the exception to this rule, and in this case that person is JV Venable. He was born to lead, and he was given the opportunity to study his gift from his time as the commander and demonstration leader of the US Air Force Thunderbirds. He led a 1,100-member combat group on flying missions in Iraq and Afghanistan, and he was an Air Force officer and fighter pilot with 26 years on the point. It is the combination of the instinctive skills and the conscious understanding of exactly what those skills are that can make someone an exceptional teacher.

What makes this book a treasure is not based on JV's accomplishments but rather on the way JV can help *you* accomplish great things. In *Breaking the Trust Barrier,* JV has successfully and clearly articulated the leadership skills necessary for you to be successful with *your* teams. How does he do this? He inspires, entertains, and motivates you through his ability to not just tell a story but to provide a clear moral to that story and tie that moral to a defined leadership action.

JV doesn't just want to tell you how to be a more effective leader; he sincerely wants you to succeed at it. He starts by getting you to look at your team and identify gaps that can cause a lack of competence. Then he walks you through the commitment you extend to those you lead, the often small acts of loyalty that further the interests of those behind you. There is a big surge of energy when, due to the trust you have created, you can lead others to take the drag from your draft.

This book offers far more than just inspirational stories that generate an idea or two. In fact, what's presented here are repeatable, step-by-step processes that are measurable and therefore implementable. In turn you learn a systematic approach to leadership that can be adapted instantly to fit virtually any situation or scenario. Seek more in the pages that follow, and you will be handsomely rewarded.

There is one learning demon that you'll need to beware of—especially if you are already a good leader. This is the voice in your head that whispers: *I'm already an effective leader. Isn't that good enough?* Being too good to learn more or to think you can't improve on your leadership skills just doesn't make sense.

When I was a 21-year-old insurance agent for New York Life, I learned an invaluable lesson that I'd like to share. It was decided that we would try filming the insurance agents and give them an opportunity to evaluate their performances. In addition, I would provide feedback. I was pretty green, but I was coached on what to look for, and I was ready to go.

A form was placed in everyone's mailbox. It spoke about this new and rare opportunity to view one's approach to selling and get some feedback. It was a mandatory exercise for all 21 of the recently hired apprentice field underwriters (AFUs) but optional for the other 57 agents. Of these 57 agents, 52 were tenured agents and five were

Chairman's Council agents—the most successful agents in the country representing the top 2.5 percent of the sales force. At the bottom of the form, to help with scheduling, it was requested that all agents respond either yes or no. What followed was something I will never forget.

Of the 78 forms that were returned, as expected all 21 AFUs requested various filming dates and times. Not one of the 52 tenured agents chose to take advantage of this learning experience, and, ironically, the only agents who wanted to participate were all five Chairman's Council agents. In other words, the top agents in the country were the only ones who wanted to learn how to be even better agents. But wait, there's more.

Many of the AFUs were a little put off by the experience, going through the motions and casually nodding at the feedback they received. When the Chairman's Council agents came through, each one had a pad of paper and never stopped asking questions and taking notes. Each of the Chairman's Council agents—five of our best in the country—came to the filming obsessed with getting better.

What those five agents taught me was that there are many common traits that successful people share. One trait that seemed of paramount importance was a desire to improve, no matter what one's current level of success might be.

Now let's apply this lesson to this book. You've accomplished the hard part; you've picked this book up. You may already be a good leader—but reading this book will help you be an even *better* leader. You'll need to think about it and digest the messages. You'll want to try to implement the lessons you will learn, and if you do that, you'll see your leadership skills improve. You'll want to thank JV Venable for writing this book because he will make you a better leader. You've come this far, now go even further and let a born leader and exceptional teacher take you further than you could ever imagine.

Preface

The most demanding and gratifying leadership role of my life was my time as the commander and demonstration leader of the United States Air Force (USAF) Thunderbirds. My selection for that position was the culmination of a lifelong dream. The passion for flying began when I was four years old, standing on the roof of our home in Fairfield, Alabama. Three Kingfisher biplanes came screaming overhead so low that I could see the pilots waving at me. I got so excited I almost fell off the roof. By the age of nine, that passion had shifted from flying, to flying fighters, to leading the Thunderbirds.

For the first dozen or so years after college, I lived a dream that few rock-and-roll stars can compete with and flew the F-16 all over the world. About the time I could apply for the commander/leader position on the Thunderbirds, I ran into a wall like few others: I was diagnosed with cancer. My family history is rife with the disease, and after a second operation I was told to prepare for the battle of my lifetime—and that I would never fly again. Putting that childhood dream back up on the horizon helped me recover from one of my biggest setbacks, and capturing the dream came through a series of miracles that I will never be able to explain. What I found when I got there exceeded every expectation I had framed through the whims of adolescence.

The annual turnover within the Thunderbirds was significant. We lost a third of our enlisted force: half the officers and, with them, half the pilots who flew the demonstration every year. That programmed attrition forced us to train a new team from the most basic level forward at the end of every demonstration season.

In just three and a half months of training, we took men and women who had never worked together and methodically developed the kind of trust that allowed them to thrive at the extremes of performance and risk. We really did trust one another with our lives, and the method the team developed to ingrain that kind of dynamic was nothing short of phenomenal. By the time I came on board, our organization had been refined by 48 generations of Thunderbird teams that streamed seamlessly into the one I led. The process that lineage passed on to our team was the best I've ever known. My goal in writing this book is to share the steps for generating trust at this level—trust that can further the nature of your team or workplace, no matter what you do.

Along the way I intend to engage a bias you may be carrying—that leading in the military is somehow different from leading in your world. Even in combat, getting people to deliver what your team needs depends on something much more than blind obedience. It relies on your deliberately building the foundational elements that compel the desire to follow. The biggest of those elements is trust.

All the stories in this book are true, and while many of the names are those of actual people, others were changed to protect individual and organizational trajectories beyond our time together. The world of the fighter pilot is big on call signs (nicknames), and you will find many in the pages that follow. Some are simple, some are creative, and some are designed to make a relatively intense occupation a little more enjoyable.

*Breaking the
Trust Barrier*

Introduction

Trust. No team or organization can excel over the long haul without it, and for many leaders the path to establishing it is anything but clear. Trust is the willingness to put yourself or your team at risk with the belief that another will follow through with a task, in a role, or with a mission. Expressions of trust that lack an element of risk are merely expressions.

Because you picked up this book, I will make some assumptions about you. You are a leader who cares about the performance and well-being of your people, but you sense that something—maybe gaps in trust or communication—are holding you and your team back. The good news is that you've taken a great step toward increasing the cohesion and performance of your team by just reading the introduction to this book. With each successive page, you will learn a bit more about a predictable, repeatable process for building trust within your team—a process that begins with an individual's desire for commitment from you and ends with his or her trust in you. Once you have finished the last page, you will see the process everywhere you turn and in every facet of your life.

I will warn you right now that there are no shortcuts or quick solutions offered herein. As a matter of fact, I will ask you to take risks and move to engage your team in ways others might consider idealistic or unnecessary, but I promise you will be rewarded for your efforts.

Biases: The Barrier to Trust

Whom do you trust, and what made you cross that threshold? Whom don't you trust, and what keeps you from believing in that person? Very often the decision comes not just from what we see but from the events and experiences stored in the processors in our heads and our hearts. Any relationship begins with an introduction, and that first impression is lasting for reasons that are often hard to understand. Consciously or unconsciously, some facet about that person matches something inside of us—something that was coded in us during adolescence or that we absorbed (or coded in ourselves) along the path of our adult lives. Call them predispositions or intuition if you'd like, but, right or wrong, biases reside in all of us.

biases

Internal layers of protection that help us resist putting our physical, emotional, or financial well-being at risk.

Biases are internal layers of protection that help us resist putting our physical, emotional, or financial well-being at risk. How you dress, act, and sound fit an internal mold in another's mind—a mold cast by a whole host of characters and events, good and bad, in their lives. Where you were raised and your culture, dialect, manners, and mannerisms match biases that directly or unconsciously shape how you view others—and how others view you. Biases form the barrier to trust we are up against as leaders.

Breaking the Trust Barrier

The challenging thing about biases is that you may never fully understand what they are in your own mind, much less in the minds of your people. With that as backdrop, there is little use in dwelling on the indicators, or rationales, for biases—we can leave them to people who study behavior. Our job as leaders is to overcome biases by building a portfolio of seamless actions and engagements that inspires our people to write new code—code that will incrementally entice them to close the trust gap.

We will talk a great deal about gaps in this book, but the critical thing to remember is that closing the gaps on trust relies on the *whole you*. It begins with your commitment to the individuals on your team—your willingness to actively engage and listen to the people you lead—and then your moving on the interests and passions you discover within those engagements to foster loyalty.

The effort you spend building commitment and loyalty will take you to the threshold, but closing beyond the trust barrier relies on pulling your team forward with your integrity and your deeply seated principles (see Breaking Through).

This book steps you through the process of closing gaps by introducing a new system of leadership called *drafting*. You have seen the aerodynamic phenomenon at work

Breaking Through: *First Commitment, Then Loyalty, and Finally Trust*

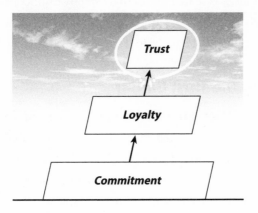

through the V formations of migratory birds, a train of speed skaters, stock car racers, and the likes, where the efficiencies and effects of teams are magnified with proximity.

My two years on the point of the Thunderbirds offered some incredible insights on trust—and the real effects and power of drafting. It was that experience—and that incredible team—that served as my inspiration for writing this book. Through 26 years of service and two tours of combat duty, I can say without reservation that every team I flew with or served on relied on trust. But as you read through each chapter, you will discover what I did about Thunderbirds: that our mission required a level of trust that few organizations will ever know or enjoy—it really was something else.

Our process for building and sustaining trust is laid out here for you and your team. Read on, take hold of the reins, and break your barriers to trust.

PART I

COMMITMENT   LOYALTY

Are There Gaps on Your Team?

A leader has three primary roles: set the direction—the vision for the team; attract and retain the best talent you can find; and build and protect the corporate culture.

–Robert Walter
Founder and Former CEO
Cardinal Health

TRUST

Leo Van Wart is a professional golfer who helped propel Notah Begay III to the ranks of the Professional Golfers Association of America. Leo was hired to run a golf complex just outside of Las Vegas, and shortly after he arrived he hopped in a golf cart and drove the expanse of his new course. Many fairways and greens were in disrepair, and the desert had all but reclaimed his new driving range. When he stopped by the grill and sampled its marquee item—a flavorless cheeseburger—he had a complete picture of why the course was bleeding money. The biggest gap he found in the operation was ownership. No one on the small team took pride of ownership in the work—there was no sense of cohesion or unity. To them the course was just a job. Does that sound familiar?

A *gap* is a physical or emotional distance caused by a lack of competence, a lack of confidence, or an unmet social need. No matter what your profession is or how impressive your team may be to an outsider, you know that there are gaps keeping your team from maximizing its potential. That is true for every organization—and it was certainly true for the Thunderbirds.

We billed ourselves as *the Air Force's number one recruiting tool,* and our books said that more than 10 million people experienced the Thunderbirds in one way or another every year. We put on an airshow that was first-rate. By all appearances the team was firing on every cylinder when I came on board, but shortly thereafter I found a few things that were hard to reconcile.

The Air Force Recruiting Service ran a series of high-profile television commercials the year I took command, and the Thunderbirds—the Air Force's number one recruiting tool—was not in a single frame. That was telling. The more I listened, the more I heard my new team complain about strained, deteriorating, or nonexistent relationships with the Air Force Recruiting Service, with our parent public affairs organization, and with other offices and agencies we should have been supporting or whose support we needed to conduct our mission.

The more I sought out the math surrounding that 10-million-people-per-year figure, the more elusive it became, and our metrics, methods, and alliances were not adding up to that powerful slogan. Positive exposure to the general public was our mission, and even under that banner you could find issues. We had endured a series of aircraft mishaps and personal conduct issues in our more recent history, which caused senior leaders to pull signature maneuvers and formations from the demonstration. The trends were clear, and our critical metrics were headed in the wrong direction.

Gaps in the Thunderbird Operation

The team was running hard, but our laser focus on operations—on flying the demonstration—allowed gaps to develop in the performance of our overall mission, and we were falling short of our real potential to reach the public. Again, from the outside we were holding our own, but we clearly had three organizational gaps in performance: outreach, complacency, and discipline.

Spotting the Gaps on Your Team

If you are new to an operation, just walking the grounds will give you a great deal of perspective. If you have been with the team for a while, get away for long enough to gain a bit of perspective, then come back and take a fresh look. As you move about, make sure you take the time to watch and listen to your people. Most of us get elevated into leadership roles on our ability to speak up, but the move to a position on point requires an adjustment. One of the best pieces of advice I received for spotting gaps was from Brigadier General Thomas "Griz" Wolters, USAF, Retired: "Never miss the opportunity to shut the [*expletive*] up." Your people will talk freely if you let them, and their words will paint a picture of the exceptional areas—and the gaps—in your operation. Once you have an assessment in hand, you can build or refine your team's goals, elevate its trajectory, and craft a plan to close the gaps to the point where you break the barrier to trust.

The Road Ahead

We ease into the process of drafting by giving you a vivid glimpse of how it all began. From there we step into the Thunderbird hangar and show you how we took people who didn't know one another and had never flown formation acrobatics before and, in a little more than three months, moved them from commitment to unqualified trust. There is a surge in momentum waiting for you just ahead, so strap yourself in and let's get started.

Draft Your Team to Trust

I t was a gorgeous day in the middle of the Thunderbirds' show season, and we were flying over some of the most breathtaking countryside I had ever seen. The radios were crisp, and from the moment we released brakes we were hitting all the marks in a compressed maneuver sequence we had been perfecting for months.

The four of us completed our reposition behind the crowd line and then stabilized for just a second. The moment we passed over those 40,000 people, I pulled the trigger on the next maneuver. The 4 G* pull that started our trail-to-diamond cloverloop stabilized, and just as we approached the vertical I called the three jets behind me to move from their trail position to our signature diamond.

At the start of training season, the distance between jets was the same as we had flown throughout our

---

*Short for *gravitational force,* or *g-force:* A measurement of the type of acceleration that causes weight; 1 G is equal to the force of gravity experienced under normal conditions. At 1 G a pilot's head and helmet weigh approximately 20 pounds. They effectively weigh 180 pounds at 9 Gs.

operational lives, but now the formations were so tight—
and the gaps between us so small—that I thought I could
feel a shift as the left and right wingmen moved into position. So far as I knew, the surge that came with Rick "Chase"
Boutwell and Jon "Skid" Greene moving into their respective formations was emotional, but it felt like they were
literally lifting the wings of my jet.

As each accelerated into position that day, a very
subtle shift took hold of our trajectory. The pressure came
on as if a giant hand were pushing up on my left wing. The
ensuing right turn began to take us away from a pure vertical loop, and, almost unconsciously, I countered with the
call for "a little left turn" and the slightest amount of pressure on the stick to bring us back on plumb.

From the crowd's perspective, this would be one of
the best demonstrations of the year, and most spectators
would leave with a level of pride that matched the wave of
exhilaration we were riding as the last jet touched down.
And yet the blemish of that trail-to-diamond cloverloop
was still lingering in the back of my mind. I knew I hadn't
consciously turned the flight, but I was at a loss as to how
the maneuver had gone wrong. After I watched the video
recording of our demonstration in the debrief, I noticed a
small difference.

My left wingman was more aggressive on his move
forward, and he tucked into position a bit more quickly
and closely than the jet on my right—and he stayed there.
He was so close that he caused my left wing to become
more efficient, to produce more lift than my right wing.
Efficiencies—it was aerodynamic efficiencies! It wasn't just
a *feeling* that I was being carried by the team around me;

the surge brought on from their proximity was *real*. That thought would change the way I looked at everything: we were *drafting*.

The Phenomenon of Drafting

The aerodynamic phenomenon of drafting was discovered in the late 1950s by stock car racers who figured out that two cars running close together, nose-to-tail, could sustain a faster speed than either car could achieve on its own. Over time they figured out the cause of the effect: the lead car was taking on the wall of air for both, while the trailer was close enough to the leader's bumper to relieve it from the drag it created as it moved down the track (see Aerodynamic Drafting).

Aerodynamic Drafting: *Closing the Gap Benefits Both Team Members*

The lead car plows a path through air. Another car trailing behind will experience less resistance and a boost in performance.

The benefits for the trailing car increase as it closes the gap on the leader. When the trailer closes inside of one car length, the leader's drag decreases, allowing that car to accelerate.

When the gap is closed, the collective effect allows a team of two cars to accelerate to a speed that neither car could achieve on its own.

While the effects are mutually beneficial, they are a little lopsided—at least at first. When a car speeds down the track, its movement plows a path through the air to create a vacuum of sorts that can help *pull* a trail car forward when it is still several car lengths behind the leader. And if the trailer *elects* to close on the leader's bumper, the pull becomes more significant with every foot of closure on the leader's car.

But, funny enough, the leader gains no relief from its drag until the trailer is within a single car length. As the trail car closes inside that distance, the leader's drag begins to transfer from its bumper to that of the trailer. When the gap closes, the collective effect allows the team of two cars to accelerate to a speed that neither car could achieve on its own. It is closing the distance—the gaps between elements on a team—that makes drafting work. The more I thought about it, the more I could see drafting's effects on the Thunderbirds everywhere I turned.

Every unit within our organization, from accounting and finance to maintenance and public affairs—literally every shop—was minimally staffed, and each relied on the others to help it execute its role. Those amazing people were lined up, bumper to bumper, taking the weight—the drag— off the individual or element in front of them while they sustained the draft for those behind them.

Drafting, in teamwork, is a phenomenon that replicates the aerodynamic benefits of bodies moving closely together. It requires leaders to inspire closure between individuals and entities to deliver cohesion, unity of effort, and team acceleration.

> ### drafting
>
> *(aerodynamics)* The phenomenon whereby two objects moving close together sustain a faster speed than either object could achieve on its own. *(teamwork)* The phenomenon inspired by the aerodynamic property of bodies moving closely together; it requires leaders to inspire closure between individuals and entities to deliver cohesion, unity of effort, and team acceleration.

Think about that in terms of you and your team. How many folks are snuggled up against your bumper, taking the drag off your efforts, and how many are sitting two car lengths back, smoking a Lucky while basking in the warmth of your draft? It is absolutely up to the folks in your wake to close the distance—you cannot *make* them close. It is up to us as leaders to set the conditions that will make them *want* to close the gaps. By incrementally building mutual commitment, then loyalty, and finally the kind of trust that will further the momentum of the whole team, we maximize the effects of drafting.

Closing the Gaps with Commitment, Loyalty, and Trust

Trust comes through a series of methodical actions that begin and end with the leader. No pilot begins the first day of his tour with the Thunderbirds flying inches away from another's wing. That kind of proximity relies on trust that is built over time. Closing those gaps must be done incrementally, through a methodical process that, more than any other facet, relies on *you*.

Before we go into the process of building trust, let's clear up one possible misconception right up front: the Thunderbirds are not all that different from your team. Certainly, some aspects of our mission made us unique, so let's get them out of the way now.

Differences from Team to Team

The Thunderbirds' flight-training program taught pilots who had never flown formation aerobatics everything from basic formations to the entire jet demonstration sequence. We started in mid-November, flying two jets, side by side, executing one maneuver over and over, 1 mile above the desert floor, with 3 feet of separation between jets. As the training progressed, we would methodically add jets and maneuver elements, lower the maneuvering floor until we had all six F-16 fighters flying maneuvers 400 feet above the ground. By the end of the training season, the gaps between aircraft were as small as 18 inches.

In mid-March the team packed up and went on the road for the next eight months to fly airshows all over the world. With the deployments, practices, airshows, and redeployments home, we flew six days a week through the middle of November. The day after we finished the last airshow, we started the team-building process all over again.

While the differences may seem stark between our operation and yours, the parallels and personalities are an absolute match. Without question, the mission of the Thunderbirds was unique and the expectations for precision were very high. But the makeup of personnel in our hangar was very similar to the composition of your team right now.

Similarities from Team to Team

Any industry in the world includes tens, hundreds, even thousands of organizations that perform the same basic task, build the same kind of equipment, or deliver the same service. Some of those organizations deliver the gold standard and always produce the very highest levels of quality within their industry. Other organizations produce solid, reliable results, and still others struggle to deliver a competent service or reliable product on time.

The difference between high-performing organizations and those that fall short of the gold standard is not just talent but how well leaders develop their team's draft with the talent they have. Your role in that process is critical, as you will not only plow the path for the people behind you to follow but also set the conditions that will compel them to close the gaps between individuals, elements, and teams—the gaps that slow you down.

Drafting Is All about Closing the Gaps

To harness the effects of drafting and bring trust to bear within your team, you need to focus on closing the gaps. As mentioned, a *gap* is physical or emotional distance caused by a lack of competence, a lack of confidence, or an unmet social need that degrades performance. Left unaddressed, gaps are momentum killers that will thwart any hope of trust.

> **gap**
> Physical or emotional distance caused by a lack of competence, a lack of confidence, or an unmet social need that degrades performance.

The explanation for team members' gaps varies with both tenure and competence. A new hire will sustain his or her distance until a level of *traction*—technical competence and social acceptance—makes it safe to close. The reasons for gaps in more seasoned individuals take longer to figure out. Even after their needs are met, the smart ones will take their time closing because, as in our demonstration, distance gives them the reaction time they need to preserve their well-being.

Proximity Narrows Focus

When flying, the closer you get to the lead jet, the greater the demand on your eyes and reflexes to keep you out of harm's way. The more you close, the quicker you must shift your eyes—your **crosscheck**—between the leader, the other jets in the formation, and the threats to your well-being, such as the ground. When you are 50 feet back, your crosscheck can be slow and methodical and still allow you to sustain safe separation from the leader throughout some pretty aggressive maneuvering. Close some of that distance, however, and your focus must intensify because the area you can cover in your crosscheck narrows. Close a bit more and you'll gain some of the aerodynamic benefits from the jet in front of you while preserving just enough reaction time to get out of Dodge if things go south.

> **crosscheck**
> Taking stock of your immediate environment by shifting your focus between two or more objects.

You have lived that distance when moving at speed during rush-hour traffic. Your focus on the bumper in front of you gives you little time to check the status and intentions of the cars to your left and right, but, in your mind, your quick reflexes will allow you to react in time to avoid hitting the car in front of you if conditions deteriorate in a hurry.

During one maneuver in our demonstration, the distance between our jets was often less than that from my elbow to the tip of my fingers. If you were driving that close while clipping along at 65 miles per hour, your focus on the car in front of you would take all of your concentration—while you hope that the car you're trailing holds its speed. Flying that close maximized the effects of our team, but it also reduced reaction times to the point where the pilots on my wing could not save their own lives if I made a catastrophic mistake. Making a living flying that close to a jet moving in all three dimensions—400 feet off the ground at 500 miles per hour—takes much more than faith or concentration; it requires the deepest levels of trust.

Our Thunderbird team spent hundreds of hours together methodically developing every reinforcing input we could collect on one another to close the gaps in our formation. The whole time we were flying over the practice range, a supervisor on the ground was grading our every maneuver. I also knew that there were five other sets of eyes flying alongside me that were watching *my* every move—watching not just how I executed the maneuvers (my job) but also every other insight they could glean in the air (and on the ground) to see how I added up. They needed to know they could trust me before they closed the gaps to the point where they put themselves at risk on my wing.

The Real Benefits of Closure

The bigger the gaps between you and your followers, the more weight you will carry. Trailers who continually show up late for work, who greet initiatives with antagonism, or who consistently meet deadlines with disappointment can thwart every effort to accelerate your team. Getting those individuals to close the gap of commitment will take that administrative weight off your plate. Draw them further forward into loyalty, and you will have solid performers who serve as advocates that positively shape the attitudes and mind-sets of the team around them. Close the gap of trust, and your empowerment of key players to handle significant efforts will give you more energy and bandwidth to elevate the trajectory of the organization behind you.

How do you close that distance? How do you get your followers to let go of whatever is holding them back? To get them to close those gaps to the point where you realize the surge of drafting, you need to develop a plan to fulfill the needs, the wants, and unfulfilled elements of their working lives. The first step in that plan, the first thing they will look for, is commitment—your commitment to their place on the team.

Drafting's First Step:
Closing the Commitment Gap

The Thunderbirds had 130 team members from 24 different job specialties and career fields throughout the Air Force—and every one of them arrived with his or her own tribal mind-set. We had all been in the Air Force prior to joining the Thunderbirds, but we had never been required to work together in a single hangar. Getting people who identified themselves as fighter pilots, engine mechanics, videographers, public affairs professionals, and the like to shed their stove-piped mind-sets and meld together as a team required a concerted effort. The first step in that process was building *commitment,* and we did that through our onboarding program.

The impressions that new hires take from the first days and weeks on your team are lasting and will affect their commitment to you and your draft throughout their tenure with the team. The single biggest factor in their long-term commitment is how much their new team values *them*—how much time and effort you are willing to invest to get them settled in, socially integrated, and technically qualified.

In some ways the more experience a team member has, the more challenging the first steps to commitment might be. Not everyone will fight new goals or course corrections, but even your hardest-working folks crave stability, and getting your people to commit to a different path can be challenging. Even military leaders holding the kind of authority their subordinates have sworn to follow face the same challenges you do in compelling their people to align on a new direction.

People will not always move based on logical reasoning, like the promise of more responsibility or a bigger compensation package, but they will always close on emotions. Your challenge lies in figuring out which emotions to tap to get your followers' commitment, as well as on your making first contact with the elements and obstacles that slow them down. My efforts to engage every aspect of that challenge began the first week of an individual's onboarding.

Being genuinely curious about the people behind you and showing interest in their challenges, goals, and dreams will get them to close on the emotion of *hope*—the hope that you will do something for them in the future. Follow through with one or two of the things you learn along the way, and you can get them to close into the lane of loyalty.

Drafting's Second Step: Closing the Loyalty Gap

Loyalty is cohesion within a relationship—the kind that can be built only on the foundation of commitment. Once your trailers know that you are committed to their well-being, they will open up and, with a little encouragement, shed their outward personas—their overt positions—and tell you about their *real* motivations and genuine passions.

> ### loyalty
> Cohesion within a relationship—the kind that can be built only on the foundation of commitment. It is fostered by a leader's willingness to go the distance to support his or her team without the expectation that they will respond in kind.

Most people have several foundational elements or *pillars* within their lives that drive their actions. At times the important pillars are obvious; at other times they are well masked. With just a little forethought, you can find a trove of information that will help you motivate your people more than any other tangible benefit you can offer. Remember, however, that the performance—and loyalty—of others is often tied to growth in areas that are not directly related to work.

The opportunity to give individuals a leg up or to bolster another central element or pillar in their lives can be a very powerful motivator. Discovering those passions and then helping individuals further them can help bring more of their potential to bear for and within the team. Once you know their passions, you will know how to reach into their chests and begin pulling them forward on their wants and needs. Do that and you'll instill a sense of your confidence in them and bring on a feeling of unity you'll both revel in. Only you, the leader, can initiate this action—and you do not want to miss it.

Building respect   Moving with the talents, and on the judgment of the people who work for you, is the first step toward empowering them to handle some of your responsibility. In the quest for opportunities to increase the exposure of the Thunderbirds to the public, our team came up with several novel ideas. While public affairs would be the central hub of our efforts, we wanted to get the entire team involved. One of the best ideas actually came from a member of our maintenance team.

Each jet had two cameras that captured spectacular cockpit footage throughout our demonstration. The cameras were there for safety, but if we could figure out a way to share that live footage on the Internet and with local television and airshow audiences, there was potential to increase the number of folks who saw any and every one of our demonstrations.

With a few guiding thoughts and no budget for the project, I asked our maintenance officer to flesh out the idea. Within a few weeks, his team had designed a system around the components of obsolete data-link equipment designed for another aircraft. Giving him my backing to move on a solution his team had dreamt up was an unmistakable sign of my confidence in him.

Once you show your key players that they have your confidence, they will shift their focus from the performance of their roles to how *you* execute *yours*. They will watch for your willingness and ability to move others on the goals you claim to hold dear. Like every other aspect of their development, your team's respect for *you* needs to be consciously developed. Inspire and reinforce that respect, and you will chamber the kind of loyalty that will last well beyond their time on the team—the kind that will pull them right up to the line of trust.

Drafting at Full Throttle: Breaking the Trust Barrier

Every year our training season culminated at the end of February. In the weeks leading up to our graduation from training, we were flying an entire 36-maneuver demonstration package 500 feet above the ground with all six jets. That altitude, coupled with the training spreads (gaps) between jets, gave every pilot enough reaction time and space to recover from an errant maneuver—but we were about to move beyond that threshold.

The conscious decision to fly even tighter formations at lower minimum altitudes—the ones we'd be flying during airshows—relied on every bit of faith and confidence we had built in one another; we knew the risks went way up from here. Closing the gaps to airshow spreads and lowering our target minimum altitude to 400 feet meant the pad was gone. If I made a catastrophic mistake in the lead aircraft, the peripherals would not allow the wingmen to recognize pending ground impact in time for them to save their own lives. Closing the final gaps and dropping down to airshow altitude required the highest levels of trust.

Trust was a big deal on the Thunderbirds. Since the team's inception in 1953, 19 men have died flying the demonstration; our lives really did depend on the other team members. Trust may just as well have been written on the inside of our visors—as we looked for it everywhere, constantly taking in every insight, every nuance, that would reinstill our belief in one another.

During our seemingly endless hours over the practice range and through the execution of thousands of maneuvers, we were slowly writing new code on one another— programming code about the people around us that we would use as the basis of trust. Every time I executed my role correctly, or fessed up after I didn't, I was shaping their insights into my character—consciously pulling them toward trust. Although we made those assessments in the air, the same thing was true for the team members on the ground.

Building trust   If it isn't already clear, your actions as a leader initiate the process of drafting, and the effort required (and the scrutiny you'll receive) is significant—but the benefits and pride that emerge when you pull your team in tight are extraordinary. This is when your people are close enough to take the weight from your wings and when the efficiencies of drafting are highest. When key members of your team are empowered, you give them your authority to take big efforts off your desk, freeing you up to plan and then elevate the trajectory of the entire team. You will move faster and accomplish more together than you ever could have done on your own.

Developing the kind of trust that leads to a Thunderbird-level of closure can be very powerful. Feeling those jets tuck in to position was as much emotional as it was physical. There is nothing more powerful or electrifying, nothing that will accelerate your team faster or make them want to stay with you longer, than building an effective draft. The secrets, techniques, and lessons that will help you lead your team to that kind of closure are detailed in the chapters that follow. Read on.

PART II

COMMITMENT

PART **II**

Commitment

Alone we can do so little. Together
we can do so much.

−Helen Keller

ommitment is the demonstrated will to deliver for the people around you. Your commitment will give people confidence and the desire to accelerate within your draft. The timing of your moves to fill those gaps is critical, as it will likely set the standard for your *followers'* commitment for the duration of their time on your team. Deliver your commitment, and the commitment of people behind you is sure to follow.

I learned a lifelong lesson about generating commitment from what was supposed to be the worst posting of my career. The assignment was to one of the most dreaded and isolated locations in the Air Force: Kunsan Air Base, Korea. Kunsan was the definition of remote, and there was every reason to avoid it. It meant a year away from family, fresh milk, television, and just about any other amenity associated with American culture. Phone calls home were $1 per minute, and it was a three-hour drive to the equivalent of a Walmart. Just the trip over on a 747 was a bone crusher, and my third leg into Korea was particularly so. After we landed,

> **commitment**
> The demonstrated will to deliver for the people around you.

those of us destined for Kunsan boarded a bus for a three-hour ride.

As we approached the final stop, folks began to move on the same advice I'd been given: "Don't be the last one off the bus!" Several began swimming through the sea of passengers to get first rights to the door. I managed to step out just ahead of the other guy headed to my unit. Mike "Hans" Gantt was on my back.

When I looked up, a group that was as engaging as I'd ever known welcomed us to "the best fighter squadron in the world," nicknamed "the Juvats." As the last guy off the bus, Hans was presented with a 4-foot-tall wooden replica of a Pacific Island headhunter. "Woody" would be his constant companion until the next new guy came on board as the last one off his bus.

After stowing our bags, we cleaned up and met at the club, where the most revered fighter pilot in the squadron told us all about the "incredible" year ahead. By the time we hit the sack that night, my outlook had done a 180. This had the potential to be the best assignment of my career. Those first moments at Kunsan were worth their weight in gold.

Most of us will move with, and commit to, those who give us what we need. Strong leaders entice us forward by filling in the gaps in front of us, even when we might not know what those gaps are. Whether it is a new hire moving to his or her first job with your company or the commitment of a seasoned professional you are trying to capture, you need to clear the obstacles that impede or hinder his or her closure on you and commitment to the team.

CHAPTER 2

Close the Traction Gap

U p to this point in your life, you have probably associated the word *traction* with the grip of your tires on a slick or icy road, but the term **traction** is equally powerful to describe—and visualize—the footing you offer new hires coming on board your team. Giving them traction means offering the technical and social footing they need to take their place in, and feel the first effects of, your draft.

> ### traction
> The footing a leader offers new hires that allows them to take their place in, and feel the first effects of, the leader's draft.

Your commitment to their onboarding process gives them the kind of traction that leads to *their* commitment.

Minimizing the time and emotional space that lies between the hiring process and giving your newest assets traction is critical to capturing their long-term engagement. Every organization has specific techniques, methods, information, and demands that will be unfamiliar to folks coming in from the outside.

Onboarding for Success

There is nothing like a little uncertainty to elevate the anxiety of a new hire's transition, and it always surprises me when a company either has no onboarding process or has one that is not very well thought out. You need to remove as much of their uncertainty as you reasonably can, and your goal should be to guide your newest team members through every step in their first few weeks with the organization. As with my experience at that remote base in Korea, enthusiasm about where you are and what you do will make the next step of closure that much easier.

You may be tempted to short-change your **onboarding program** and let your new hires fend for themselves, but I can speak firsthand to the repercussions of dropping that ball because I have lived through them myself.

> **onboarding program**
>
> The program or process teams offer new hires to orient them to their new environment and to give them the technical and social footing they need to take their place on the team.

Stepping into a Nightmare

My assignment to the Pentagon came at a point when I was a seasoned officer but an unqualified novice in the mechanisms and tribalism within "The Building." We in the military are famous for acronyms and abbreviations, but that place operates at a whole different level. My new boss's first direction, "Follow the JACO to 4D250 and brief A5XS on J8's JCDE initiative for JCIDS," was a flashback to the Pompendu nightmare—my eighth-grade French teacher who refused to speak English in our introductory class. I had no clue what either of them was talking about.

Looking back, I think Mrs. Pompendu may have designed my new team's onboarding campaign: no formal or informal welcome, no orientation, no secret decoder ring for Pentagonese, no cheat sheet for job titles or office designations, not even helpful hints on how to navigate the puzzlelike corridors of that massive office structure. This was a completely different experience from the one I enjoyed in Korea, and my only option was to fight through it and learn by immersion.

The next several months were as foreign to me as they were exhausting, and my efforts to gain traction would have been more effective in a warm vat of tar. Getting out of bed every morning was drudgery, and I shook my head in disbelief all the way home each night.

Unfortunately, that kind of experience is not limited to the Pentagon. If you are like most, you have very likely spent months fighting for some semblance of traction in a new job, all the while questioning your own sanity for joining that team. You were able to sustain your commitment through the transition, but if you think back on the challenges, it is easy to see how others with less fortitude could get beaten down to the point where they quit or (worse) become actively disengaged.

Most will fight the good fight to gain proficiency and assimilate into your team, but the whole time that they are trying to gain footing, they will be building their case for or against committing to *you*. If we as leaders don't give new hires our genuine interest, time, and a leg up on gaining

traction, we may very well lose them to another organization or to a distracted state within our own.

Your actions to help your new hires settle in need to be
well timed and targeted. You will want to give them insights
into the challenges and questions you faced so long ago that
you may have forgotten just how pressing they were. For
those relocating to join you, your engagement will actively
further much more than their search for living quarters.
You can help shape their attitude and energy level in a way
that will affect every other facet of their new circumstances.
This stage for developing commitment is critical and
involves every aspect of settling in to a new environment.

Thunderbird Onboarding

By the time I came on the team, the onboarding program
for the Thunderbirds was a full 21 days. Airmen (this
term applies to both men and women in the Air Force)
who fought long and hard to get a place on the team wore
patches from their previous units until they completed the
program. That made them easy for the rest of the team—
the *old heads*—to spot. Over those three weeks, the new
hires would spend a lot of time learning the ins and outs of
their new world by memorizing the Thunderbirds' onboarding handbook. Their shepherds assigned them tasks to
familiarize them with our mission and facility and to force
them to get to know every member of the team.

Those who joined the Thunderbirds would employ
their well-honed professional skills on the team, although
our operation was completely different from the one they
had known. A fighter unit might be expected to deploy
once or twice a year, and those moves followed months

of planning and logistical preparation. Our operation deployed to a new employment location at least once a week for eight straight months and involved giving new hires an understanding of how they fit into that process. That alone was worthy of its own onboarding program, but there was another area most of us had never experienced.

As the team went from show site to show site, anyone wearing our uniform was peppered with questions about life on the Thunderbirds and in the Air Force: "What kind of gas do those jets burn?" "How many shows do you guys fly a year?" "How many pilots have died flying with the team?" Our hangar had been turned into a working museum over the years, and, even when we were home, every team member would be a spokesperson for our service. They didn't need just the information; they needed training on how to deliver it in a way that furthered the Thunderbirds' mission.

To cement this training, we made it challenging—and fun. We had checkpoints—oral quizzes—at the 10- and 20-day milestones in the program; if the new hires passed both, they earned the right to meet the Thunderbird commander on the floor of the squadron hangar, where I would ask them questions. The entire team surrounded the new hires during this last hurdle, and it was a raucous event not without some innocent pranks (some team members specialized in shouting out wrong or funny answers to the easiest questions). Once the new hires passed that test, we pinned a big, beautiful squadron patch on them and welcomed them into the unit right there. It was a welcome most would cherish for the rest of their lives.

Your program will very likely be much smaller, but you must be sure to cover everything your newest people need to gain confidence and traction in their roles. The initial investment of time you expend onboarding your new people may seem outsized, but you will do more than save time and money by forgoing it—you'll leave an indelible, *negative* impression.

Don't Be That Person

On my first day on the job in one of the city's "Best Places to Work," I was filled with excitement. After 16 moves and at least as many onboarding events in the Air Force, I was about to experience how one of the very best companies in Washington, DC, did it. Human resources covered legal formalities, security badging, and time logging with impressive effect. While still holding my anticipation, I was a little taken aback when my briefer told me, "That's it—welcome aboard!" From there I was escorted to my boss's office for our first formal meeting.

He greeted me with warmth and excitement and, after exchanging a few pleasantries, moved right into the task at hand. It was a request for proposal (RFP) issued by the government, and I was just the guy who would win it for our division. My new boss handed me a copy of the RFP and suggested the names of two people in other divisions who might be willing to offer some assistance. With a pat on the back, I was sent off to complete an unfamiliar task three hours into my first day on the job.

The first lead took me to a division head, who vaguely remembered responding to an RFP, but it had been years before, and he somehow couldn't find a copy of the company's submission. He was interested in the details of the RFP, but he frankly didn't have time to offer much help. The second lead was in yet another division, and she was a bit more direct. After skimming the RFP, she caustically informed me that my division didn't even have the faculties required to work the contract if we won it. And, no, she didn't have any proposal examples she could share with me. It was quite a welcome.

There was no training, no template, and not even an example of a winning (or losing) proposal to guide my writing efforts. I had invented or reinvented the wheel for tasks and processes many times before, and knew I would make the proposal happen, so that wasn't the issue. It was the indelible impressions of the day that were hard to shake.

The day's exploration did help me become familiar with the company's organizational structure, culture, and sense of teamwork, but the firm certainly wasn't living up to its "Best Place to Work" label. My new company was actually a collection of predatory fiefdoms, and my boss either didn't care enough about me or know enough about our business to get me the training I needed to gain momentum.

We eventually won that contract, but we lost an incredible opportunity in the process. Traction and social integration give an individual momentum and the desire for *closure*. Because I had to plow my own path and I was all but backhanded in my attempts to gain any semblance of traction, my boss

> **closure**
>
> Narrowing a gap between objects (planes, entities, or people) physically or psychologically.

gave me no reason to close the gaps that would further his draft.

Technical Top-Off

I was transitioning into a completely new world in that "Best Place to Work," and the need for additional training or a technical *spin-up* should have been obvious. But most companies don't onboard folks making such big transitions, and it's easy to convince ourselves that people transitioning within our industry don't need a technical spin-up. Whether your profession is in sales, food service, or aviation, you need to give your new hires the nuances of operating in their new environment. That was certainly true with the Thunderbirds.

> **spin-up**
> To bring new hires up to speed with the tempo and technical faculties required in their jobs.

Several jobs in the hangar required significant time and resources to train new hires and bring them up to the team's performance standards. None of the pilots, for example, had ever flown aerobatics in formation, and that spin-up required quite an effort. The building-block approach we used began with just two jets flying one or two new maneuvers on each sortie. We slowly added maneuvers and aircraft to the mix until we had all six jets executing an entire demonstration together, and that process took several months. Although your program is different, you still need to make sure you cover everything your new hires need to gain traction and be confident in their jobs.

Your technical top-off program The cost and effort associated with a technical spin-up can be enough to dissuade you from building it into your onboarding program—but don't let it. Morale aside, I would have served my boss at the Pentagon much better if she had taken the time to give me a little traction. No matter what you do or how badly you need your new guys at work *right away,* your team will get much more out of your new hires much faster if you take the time to bring them up to speed with any additional or technical training they may need.

The specific training and topics you need to cover vary by organization and industry, but they are easy to outline. Ask people who have been on your team for a year what they wish they had known during their first weeks on the job, and you can start to frame your program. Once you have the framework, task one of your more energetic folks to put flesh on those bones. With a few guiding thoughts on time and resources, he or she can build (and then shepherd) the technical spin-up program for you.

There are two seemingly innocuous but remarkable elements of successful technical spin-up programs that you need to consider: make new hires easy to spot, and make their names easy to remember.

Remember Woody, the headhunter replica? Hans Gantt was impossible to miss while he toted that wooden warrior into a room, and with it he became an instant celebrity. Recall that the unit's nickname was the Juvats, and new guys were referred to as "any Juvat"—or "AJ" for short. When Hans walked in, everyone would yell, "Hey, AJ!" That instant recognition would evoke memories

of their own transitions with gusto, which brings up
the second point.

Some organizations use nametags to make fresh
recruits stand out. This is a step in the right direction, but
glancing down at a name like Håkon Hjort can make your
old heads uncomfortable enough to hamstring the effort.
If you give your new hires a generic, introductory nickname, you will remove that barrier and add a little fun.

You want to draw the name out of your organization
if you can, as we did with AJ in the Juvats, but that won't
always resonate. The sports world calls them "rookies,"
ranch hands call them "greenhorns," and in the *big* Air
Force we called them "new guys." Anything you can come
up with will work so long as everyone on the team knows
the nickname and it is not demeaning.

Making our new hires easy to spot was the perfect
icebreaker, and giving them fun, easy-to-remember nicknames made the process enjoyable for everyone. As you
might imagine, after the old heads exchanged stories with
the new guys, the care factor went up and they took time
to ensure that their new protégés mastered every required
technical skill. Those two elements were the first steps
in integrating the new hires into the social fabric of the
organization.

Integrating New Hires Socially

Any big organization like the Air Force is filled with lanes or
tribes that rarely, if ever, work together. The Thunderbirds
were unique in that regard because our mission forced
members from 24 different tribes onto a single team. We
had electricians, fighter pilots, videographers, graphic

artists, public affairs specialists, jet engine mechanics, ejection seat technicians, and 17 other career fields all working together under one roof. Each career field had its own developmental path, its own ways and methods of executing similar chores, and its own well-developed and entrenched culture. Many of the folks we hired had never had the chance to engage with more than one or two other tribes in their careers.

Getting high-end performers from each of those tribes to not only work together but also form bonds that could endure the highs and lows of our demonstration schedule was no small challenge. It meant not just spinning them up technically but integrating every new member into the social fiber of the organization.

The Thunderbirds' 21-day onboarding program included formal hurdles and embedded chores whose sole purpose was to develop social connective tissue by forcing new teammates to interact. There were times when team members from every specialty in the hangar had to rely on others to execute their technical roles. And because we relied on all hands to accomplish the chores required to move the team from one location to another, we had to have something much more than cross-departmental harmony. Ingraining interdependencies into team members began during those first weeks of onboarding.

We did our best to pair new hires for the duration of the three-week program. Having someone to share the chores, book study, and pressure associated with assimilating into a new organization makes a challenging process a little easier, and it enables their first real connection—a bond with another new hire.

The connection with the rest of the team began with our meet-and-greet sheets. New hires had to collect the initials of every member of the team—all 130 of us—during their first days in the Thunderbird hangar. The sheets forced exchanges that otherwise may never have taken place, exchanges that directly affected the new hires' assimilation. Everyone knew what it was like to step on board, and the established members of the team went out of their way to engage the new folks during these brief but very personal interactions.

Having rituals that work   We had a long list of *rituals* that brought the team together, and we introduced our new guys to them one by one. One of the biggest recurring events came with the squadron coin we gave them moments after they earned their squadron patch. It was a token that signified their place in the Thunderbird tribe. No matter where they were, if they were challenged to produce their coin by another team member and didn't, they owed that

> **ritual**
>
> A recurring event that brings the team together; it should be simple, sustainable, all-inclusive, and always elevating.

Thunderbird (and any other who was present) a beverage of his or her choice. If the challengee produced his coin, the one who made the challenge had to buy. Either way, it was a fun, simple practice that brought people together.

Rituals certainly are part of military life, but don't think they won't work for you out in the *real* world. No matter what your profession, with very little effort you can weave rituals into your team that will deliver the kind of unity that sets you above the competition.

Do You Have What It Takes to Be a Gentle Giant?

It started when Larry O'Toole hired members of a college rowing team for summer work with his moving company. The rowers liked to stay in shape by running the Harvard stadium stairs, and their outgoing nature drew other employees of O'Toole's company into the routine.

Over time the ritual became part of the onboarding process and delivered a few unintended dividends. In O'Toole's words, "A lot of people who come here have heard about the stadium, and it tells them this is the kind of place they're looking for. Some come from other moving companies, and they're tired of working with layabouts. They want to work hard and challenge themselves. And they want to do it with people who feel the same way."*

What started out as a habit of a few expanded into an effective recruiting tool and bonding mechanism in an industry known for neither. While O'Toole's brilliant move may seem like happenstance, the best ideas come from within the team rather than from on high. His genius was taking the spark from another and throwing a little kindling on it.

Don't think you have to generate every idea that drives morale. Watch for bonding opportunities that emerge in everyday life on your team and then throw your weight behind them. Once your ritual is in place, all you have to

---

*Leigh Buchanan, "Bizarre Hiring Rituals," *Inc.*, 1 March 2010.

do is tend the flames of exuberance to make sure that it continues to *elevate* every member of your team.

Devising new rituals   Every Thunderbird team ritual had four features: it was simple, sustainable, all-inclusive, and always elevating. Most organizations have operational tempos that squeeze every moment out of the working day, leaving little time or effort for building morale. By making rituals simple to execute and sustainable with regard to time and money, you factor cost out of the morale equation.

The public finale of our 21-day onboarding program was a ritual in itself for everyone on the team. It consumed no more than 20 minutes in any week, and every Thunderbird in the hangar made a point to be there. The event certainly gave team members a great view of each new hire's formal entry onto the team, but they didn't attend just for him. The event was special in that it made us remember the excitement of being introduced to the team of a lifetime. It rejuvenated us and intensified our sense of belonging. It was, by definition, elevating.

Your Program for Traction

An effective onboarding process need not be elaborate, but it does need to include every element your newest and most important acquisitions need to gain traction. When you seamlessly deliver a smooth onboarding, provide a nimble technical spin-up, and socially integrate the new hires into the team, they will feel your commitment. Once they do, the door will be open to move them toward your team goals by furthering the drivers, motivations, and gaps within their personal lives—through your direct engagement.

Here are the takeaways for designing and implementing your onboarding process for commitment:

▶ Plan on being personally involved with your new hires' onboarding process. Mass briefings alone just don't cut it.

▶ Make sure someone is with the new hire during the transitions from every step of onboarding training.

▶ Be sure to discuss the social do's and don'ts within your tribe, including the expectations and rites of passage the new hire can expect during the first months on the team.

▶ Devise a ritual or rite of passage that allows the entire team to welcome the new hire, and present a token that seals his or her place in the tribe. The Thunderbirds cherished the patch they earned through onboarding. What inexpensive keepsake will you give your new folks to seal the deal?

CHAPTER 3

Close the Engagement Gap

Getting the people behind you to close the gaps on commitment requires that they buy into the direction and supporting goals you set. People will not always close on the promise of greater salaries, benefits, or responsibilities, but they will always move on emotions. The key is finding which ones to pull on to get them to close within your draft, and figuring that out requires *your* engagement. Engage them effectively, and your people will commit.

In an age when we strive for greater and greater efficiencies and champion remote work, it is easy to put engaging the established folks in your organization low on your priority list. But the power of one-on-one **engagements**—your very presence with the people on your wing—is remarkable. When you give the individuals behind you *your* presence, you will glean insights about them and the organization that will help you entice them forward in your draft. Sometimes those things are

> **engagement**
> Your presence and one-on-one interactions with the people on your team.

obvious, and at other times, not so much. The following is a case in point.

Nik Ripken was a missionary in Somaliland during the 1990s, and he witnessed firsthand the deprivations that many Somalis suffered. When people came to his team's aid station, they were often in very bad shape. Ripken offered the obvious essentials he thought they needed—clean water, food, medical care, shelter—but somewhere along the line he realized he was still missing the mark:

> What they wanted even more, however, was for someone . . . to sit for a while, or just stand with them, and let them share their stories. . . . I was amazed to see the power of human presence. . . .
>
> By doing that, we were saying to them that they mattered. We were saying that they were important enough to be heard.*

If the presence of a stranger can have such a big impact in that environment, what kind of influence could *your* presence have on the people within your draft? Whether you are closing the gaps on someone fresh out of onboarding or pulling a little closer someone who has been on the team for years, engagement begins with your presence.

Establishing Your Presence

There are several dynamics of human presence, but two actions pave the way for all the others: capturing names and

---

*Nik Ripken, *The Insanity of God: A True Story of Faith Resurrected* (Nashville: B&H Publishing, 2013), 86, 87.

listening willingly. Names are a handhold on people's lives.
There is nothing more enjoyable or gratifying than hearing
your name being called by another—especially your boss.*

I spent time on the Thunderbirds' website to get a leg
up on the members' names before joining the team, and as
I walked toward the hangar on my first day, I recognized
Technical Sergeant Dee Denzer. "Dee, isn't it?" was met with
such a broad smile that it lit us both up. It didn't take long
for word of our conversation to spread, and as I met the
other members, all waited to find out if I knew *their* names.
Every handshake came with an opportunity to engage the
second dynamic of presence: the willingness to listen.

Capturing Names and Listening Willingly

Capturing names is a skillset you can learn, but you'll have
to dig deeper to fully engage your people: you have to *really
listen.* The connection, the glue that bonds you to your
followers, deepens when you take the time to genuinely hear
what they have to say. Listening will certainly enable you to
find the great goods within and the adjustments required
to make your operation even better. But you will also hear
the details of your followers' lives, what is important to
them, and what you have in common. Those details lay the
foundation for the rest of your time together.

Listening for a shared interest in your followers'
passions will allow you to develop a relationship through
conversation. Sports, music, movies, even poetry are easy
connections that can help you develop the rapport that will

---

*James L. Venable Sr., advice to a son about people.

encourage trailers forward in your draft. It's all about building that connective tissue.

A Presidential Approach

During the first months of 2000, former president George H. W. Bush came into the Thunderbird hangar to meet the team. When I suggested bringing the group down to the floor of the hangar, he said he would rather meet them where they were. So, we walked into the offices and cubicles of every member of the team that afternoon, where the former president met all 130 of us. After I made each introduction, he took hold of the conversation:

"Where are you from?"

"San Diego, sir."

"I love that city. It has one of my favorite Mexican restaurants in the world. Mike, have you ever eaten at El Indio, just south of Old Town?"

"It's one of my favorites too, sir!"

Bush met every person on the team that day, called us by name, and, to our amazement, found a point of commonality with every one of us. Perhaps what impressed me more than anything else was the fact that he cared enough to listen.

Meet your followers where they are, listen for a common thread, and call them by name, and you will have a live wire for engagement. Once the connection is in place and they know you are listening, it's time to encourage them forward.

Listening for Effect

Most people have several foundational pillars in their lives that drive their actions. Their dreams, aspirations, concerns, and passions extend from one of the five major areas of their lives: faith, family, friends, health, and work. At times the important pillars are quite evident; other times they are well masked. With just a little forethought, you can find a wealth of information that will help you motivate your people more than any tangible benefit you can offer.

For example, during my first conversations with our team's flight surgeon, Jay "Bones" Flottmann, he gave me the standard lines about why he joined the team but offered few details about his life beyond the fact that he was happy to be the team's doctor. I told him I had known several physicians and found them to come in one of two flavors: those who were so smart growing up that people told them, "You really need to be a doctor," and a second group who were also really smart but who grew up wanting to help people. I asked him, "Which one are you?"

Bones hesitated for a moment, then said, "I'm probably more of the first type."

"Well, what do you *really* want to do?"

"I want to fly fighters—as a pilot."

Our service had a very small program for doctors who were also operational pilots, and before I had all of those words out of my mouth, he started beaming. He was not looking for a guarantee that we could get him into that program, but by showing my interest I found out what was most important to him. With that I could begin the process of pulling Bones forward.

Just by being curious about the wants, needs, and passions of your people, you can give them the will to close whatever gaps exist between you and move them to perform in a way even *they* hadn't imagined. Use an approach to get them to open up about their lives and then listen—*genuinely listen;* when they open up, you will hear what's important. Listening really comes down to letting your people know that they matter to you.

Once the individuals on your team know that they matter, once you have shown your genuine interest, you can begin closing the gaps and moving together toward your organizational goals.

Enticing Organizational Goal Engagement

Just as with your organization's mission, the job of the Thunderbirds was clear, but knowing what you do is not enough. If you go out of your way to hire the best talent, you must challenge them with goals that will stretch their faculties. Without big goals, elite talent are prone to distractions. Some will use their brilliance to meddle outside their lane, others will work their next job, and still others will press every boundary they can find.

Using Goals to Drive Behavior

For the Thunderbirds, pushing those boundaries meant flying a little closer, flying a little lower, or maybe enjoying a few more minutes at the bar than we had the night before. We had endured a series of off-duty incidents and aircraft mishaps that could have tarnished the team's brand. Our primary role was to project to the public the highest professional image of the Air Force, and any one of those incidents could have built a barrier to trust that extended well beyond the confines of our hangar. It was obvious that the team had some distractions, and we needed a set of goals that would challenge and connect everyone.

Our mission-related goal   The mission of the Thunderbirds was to take the Air Force out to the general public, give them a glimpse of what we were all about, and then entice a select few to join our ranks. We were capable of reaching a much bigger audience—and the team had a couple of unusual stories that would draw the media to us to make that happen.

After bouncing a few ideas around, we landed on the goal of reaching 20 million people in a single year. If we hit 20 million, in my mind, we would not be doubling our 10-million-a-year slogan; we'd be increasing our real exposure numbers by a factor of three if not four. Getting there would require the efforts of the entire team, and it would take key individuals to lead supporting efforts in public affairs, maintenance, and operations. If I could entice their closure, that big number would be within reach. We put 20 million on the horizon as our goal for meeting the public.

The second goal was a bit of a Trojan horse. The air demonstration was powerful, but several repositions for follow-on maneuvers took the team 4 to 5 miles away from the field. That left periods of dead time when nothing was happening in front of the people in the stands. Compressing the maneuver sequence from 42 minutes to 30 would keep the crowd's attention—and it would more than keep ours.

It would force us to maneuver almost constantly and ward off the temptation for the pilots on my wing to press inside their positional boundaries in the formation.

Sometimes just getting your people to hear goals—much less act on them—is a big enough challenge. There are a million reasons why people don't always register what is said. Every mind has closets and trapdoors that can open in a heartbeat: problems at home, excitement about a pending vacation, or maybe one of your own brilliant lines that triggered a temporary loss of attention. In that environment, how do you raise the odds that your folks will hear and actually *move on* your team's objectives?

Goal Tending with an Emotional Hook

If you want your goals to stick, if you want your people to align behind you and move on your words, you need to create an **emotional hook**. Emotions are feelings so powerful they can shape the mental states of people around you and actually drive their behavior. The secret is picking the right emotion to tug on to get them to close the gaps in your draft.

> **emotional hook**
> An emotion that lives or is inspired to exist in an individual that is so powerful that it drives his or her behavior.

One of our team's many traits was the feeling of pride. Everyone had fought hard to be a Thunderbird, and most would have given up a stripe or promotion to stay. We owned stock in the organization—the kind that you never want to sell. Most assumed that our blue-chip brand was on track and that even with an occasional downturn we would always be well valued. If the teammates were going to accept a change in direction, they needed a clear picture of just how tenuous our valuation was. Building that tension and a sense of urgency would be my role during the first all-hands meeting of my command.

My first all-hands meeting   The commander's call took place in our auditorium, and I kicked it off with the surge of pride I felt just being part of the team. I moved methodically into the Thunderbird-free Air Force recruiting commercials that were such a sore point with the team. I then listed several other indications and concerns the team had voiced: our crowd counts were stagnant (at best), and our relationships with the public affairs shop and the Air Force Recruiting Service were all but nonexistent. The only people still buying our motto, *the Air Force's number one recruiting tool,* seemed to be the folks inside our hangar.

Our history of pushing our own limits in the air didn't result just in paint marks that could be buffed out. Some of the more recent incidents were significant, and one mishap grounded the team for four weeks in the middle of an eight-month airshow season. We had lost our signature diamond formation take-off the previous year, and the leadership above the squadron had removed a maneuver or formation during each of the previous seasons. Although that was a point of aggravation for the team, they didn't see the trend.

I went on to read aloud two congressional investigations into claims of a corrupted culture, filed by spouses of former teammates. How many more incidents or letters would it take to put the team's status in jeopardy? We were treading water with the confidence of our leadership, and we could not afford to lose that of the public.

In 1982 the four jets of the Thunderbird diamond crashed during a practice at Indian Springs, Nevada, killing all four pilots. The incident was so tragic that it almost disbanded the team for good. The Thunderbirds had supporters, but there were many others arguing for the team's dissolution, some of whom were senior leaders in the Air Force. One of their biggest arguments was about cost— the burden the Air Force carried by having a demonstration team. Were we actually worth the cost?

Pulling the individual incidents, broken relationships, and disciplinary actions into a complete picture was all it took. You could have heard a pin drop when I was done building the case for change. The emotional hook was set, and the team was ready to move on a new trajectory.

Our stock had every element associated with a blue-chip brand, but we needed to be sure the market knew we were a solid bet. To make that happen, we had to restore trust inside and outside the organization by following every regulation, directive, and guideline to the letter. The last of our goals was *to capture the confidence of kings*—by living inside the lines.

Goals for Your Team

Your assessment will reveal the gaps and unused capacity that exist within your team, and, at an absolute minimum, your goal set should challenge that remaining untapped potential. Even if your evaluation reveals that the team is running as hard as it can, big, bold goals can redefine the underlying objectives and compel your people to refine or jettison unproductive efforts or territory. Once you have your goals, convey them to your team in a way that gives them cause to align behind you.

Setting Your Emotional Hook

Keep the need for an emotional hook in mind, and as you go through your daily routine, you will eventually have an epiphany about which emotion to pull on. It will come even if your organization is filled with more part-time employees than stockholders.

A golfer's epiphany   Golf pro Leo Van Wart had seen more than a few blights when he surveyed his new golf course back in part I. While still chewing on the remnants of a flavorless, overcooked cheeseburger from his grill, an idea hit him. He walked through the double doors that led into the kitchen and, with an expression of deep satisfaction, looked at his two cooks and said, "Fellas, this has *gotta* be the best cheeseburger I've ever tasted. The only thing standing between us and great success is a little advertising. For the next six months, I'm going to tell everyone in the city of Las Vegas that the best cheeseburger in town is made right here."

True to his word, Leo walked out of that grill and started his "best cheeseburger in town" campaign. He said it everywhere he went and, to the dismay of his staff, it started working. One by one folks would step up to the grill and say, "I hear *you* make the best cheeseburgers in town, and I've got to try one!" Imagine the cooks' hearing that over and over and then watching those same folks glare in frustration as they finish their mediocre meals.

Customers voiced their disappointment to the bartenders, the starter, the pro shop, and the driving-range attendants—literally everyone who worked at that course felt the emotional surge Leo had so deftly generated. And he was relentless—as positive with his staff as he was when he was out telling every new face he met about the best cheeseburger in town.

Leo's team probably noticed the gradual decline in customer traffic, but few of them recognized or showed any concern that the course was operating in the red. They didn't care because to them it was just a job. There was no sense of belonging, no feeling of unity, no pride of ownership in the entire golf complex. Even so, how many times could his cooks meet great expectations with subpar offerings before their pride drove them back to the grill to figure out how to measure up?

Leo began turning the performance of the entire golf complex around what appeared to be the want of a better cheeseburger—but his goals were much bigger than that. He wanted to improve every aspect of the course to the point where locals would quit referring to the track as *that* course and start calling it *our* course. He knew that a radical shift in his clients' mind-sets would not occur until his team adopted the mind-set—and the course—for themselves. If he could get his cooks to catch the drive for excellence, he could entice the other key players to line up behind him. The emotional hook he used to drive those two men back to the grill was their own pride—and it worked.

Carving the Path for Closure

Once you have set the direction for your organization, your goals are put in place, and the team is engaged behind you, your job is to carve the path for their closure. Your every effort to that end will give them momentum and strengthen your draft.

CHAPTER 4

Plow the Path

The best way to spur your team into action is by carving a path for them to follow and pulling them forward in your wake. Nothing is more demotivating to a team than a leader who sets high goals, walks away, and merely expects things to happen. You will never break the trust barrier that way. You need to get out on point, engage the elements, and make first contact with the things that slow your team down.

Barriers to goals can be physical or intangible, within or beyond your organization. They can stop you dead in your tracks or stymie your team to the point that they lose all will to accelerate. Watching your operation will expose many of those barriers, but nothing works as well as asking your team directly.

If we did it right, doubling the Thunderbirds' yearly audience would involve every component within our organization. The plan to meet that 20-million goal framed the supporting efforts of our maintenance, operations, and public affairs shops.

The idea with the greatest potential for a long-term increase in our exposure was to stream live video of our airshows over the Internet. We already video-recorded every demonstration to facilitate debriefings, and, though it would not be easy, we could establish a link from our ground camera to what we envisioned as a portable video control station. Our maintenance team rapidly expanded the idea to integrate live cockpit video from the six jets flying in the demonstration. If we did it right, we could offer the same live feed to local TV stations and Jumbotrons (huge video displays) at every airshow site.

The details, requirements, and roadblocks for the effort needed to be fleshed out, but if it were doable, our maintenance and communications personnel would make it happen. Both groups were enthusiastic about the challenge. From my perspective, there didn't appear to be any internal barriers to the initiative. Our maintenance officer, Stacey "Hawk" Hawkins, volunteered to run the external traps* and then get back to me with what he found.

Internal Barriers to Engagement

I had already engaged our public affairs team leader, Guy Hunneyman, about the initiative to double our public audience. When he enlisted his staff to expand on the idea, we ran into our first significant barrier: all five members of Guy's team had more time and experience in public affairs than he did, and they pushed back hard.

Running the external traps refers to testing the waters to see if a program you want is viable and if you can garner enough support to make it happen.

Guy and I had already framed three approaches that, if successful, would culminate in doubling our numbers:

▶ Get two feature stories on major TV news magazines.

▶ Land a cereal box that featured our team.

▶ Develop advertising and public relations opportunities at show sites during the week leading up to every airshow.

His staff's response was well short of positive: "The Thunderbird story has already been told on every major TV network." "No one will give us a cereal box—we've tried it, and they're just not interested." "We don't have people or money to develop show sites, besides—it's *their* job." They could not offer details on their previous outreach attempts or the status of their marketing funds, which was telling. Our first barrier was internal.

People aren't naturally lazy, but even your hardest-working folks crave stability. There's nothing like going to a job you have mastered, and for many people mastery relies on things remaining relatively constant. Even a subtle shift in routine can cause the best on your team to dig in. Moving our hardworking public affairs shop even slightly off their established course would take quite an effort, and I would rely on their boss to develop the draft that would close those gaps.

The one external issue Guy emphasized during our conversation was our dysfunctional relationship with our parent public affairs organization. Any national initiative for media exposure would take their approval, and they would not even take our calls.

External Barriers to Engagement

Your team's insights are critical, and at times just asking their opinion can unleash a wave of energy on the simple idea that you will actually step in to clear the way for the team behind you. I took some notes during our public affairs team discussion and proceeded to my first engagement.

The classic methods for overcoming barriers are to go around them, over them, or through them. Although there are appropriate times for each of those tactics, the first and often *only* approach you need is to engage. I got in a jet and flew 2,100 miles to see the director of our command's public affairs team.

When I arrived his secretary asked me to wait in a small room. When the director entered, he wouldn't even look at me. Surreally, he sat down in the chair next to mine while staring straight out the window in front of him. He initiated more of a lecture than a conversation, with the words "Let me tell you what *your* problem is . . ."

"You mean 'our problem'—don't you, sir?"

His expression softened, and he turned, looked me in the eye, and said, "Well, yes. I guess I do."

I have no idea how or when the animosity had developed, but it melted away with a single line of concession. The ensuing conversation was more productive than either of us could have hoped. It didn't eliminate all the unhealthy friction between our organizations, but it did reopen the lines of communication—lines our public affairs team would need to get our exposure-generating efforts off the ground. That small success let our public affairs experts know that I was serious about clearing their path, and even with their reluctance it pulled them forward. We were one step closer to breaking their barrier to trust.

Plowing the Path for Your Team

Insights on the barriers impeding your team can come from anyone within your draft, but make sure you spend time running the traps with the people who will be leading the efforts. When your team sees you meeting blocking mechanisms head-on, you'll do more than just generate momentum. Your movement will carve a path and create a void—a vacuum in your wake—that will help them close within the path you've created. You will have earned their commitment, and with just a little more effort you can pull them forward into the lane of loyalty.

PART III

PART III

Loyalty

A leader is a dealer in hope.

—Napoleon Bonaparte

Loyalty is fostered by your willingness to go the distance to support your team without the expectation that they will respond in kind. Loyalty can be built only on the foundation of commitment, and while it's still one step short of trust, it offers a powerful pull forward in the concept of drafting. Your team members need to believe—in their bones—that you will guide and support them on the road ahead. I was given a great lesson in loyalty early one morning by one of the greatest leaders I have ever had the pleasure of knowing.

I had spent most of the past two weeks helping prepare our squadron for a major operational evaluation. The work was tedious, and at the end of an all-nighter I was tired, hungry, and a little out of sorts. I had been named one of four team supervisors for our unit and charged with the care and feeding of seven pilots. As the youngest supervisor, I watched the three old heads petition to get their folks into upgrade training and key positions. I was surprised and frequently disappointed by their moves to elevate their people well before I thought they were ready. It was a question of standards. As tired as I was that morning, I could not help but wonder if *my* standards were out of line—if I was holding my people back unnecessarily by not following suit.

The thought continued to eat at me as I walked by our commander's office. Lieutenant Colonel John "John-Boy" Craig was already at his desk. After pausing two steps beyond his door, I turned back, knocked lightly, and asked if he had a moment to offer a little advice. After listening to my quandary, he stared at his desk long enough for me to question my move. But what he said next would stay with me for the rest of my career: "I didn't hire you to be like everybody else. Anything else on your mind?"

John-Boy sustained his loyalty to the other three supervisors that morning, but those simple words were powerful. He conveyed his belief in me—and his loyalty to me—even when I didn't know to believe in myself.

Winning the loyalty of your team is achieved through small acts like that—acts that further the interests and passions of those behind you. You need to know what those interests are, and the onus is on *you* to take the time to learn more about the real drivers and motivations in your people's lives. When you figure them out and move to fill the needs or gaps, you pave the way for their closure in your draft.

Stoking the fires of your trailers' loyalty means helping them grow in their passions, giving them your confidence, and developing their respect. As with commitment, you need to close those gaps incrementally. The first step in that process is to engage your followers in a way that enables them to reveal their passions and accept your willingness to help them grow.

CHAPTER 5

Close the Passion Gap

Developing loyalty requires a foundation of mutual commitment, but the magic of loyalty relies on your getting to *really know* your people and what makes them tick. This is a facet of leadership that many forgo for a variety of reasons. Some leaders see "people issues" as messy and time-consuming in a world that constantly demands greater and greater efficiencies. Others believe that getting to know their teams too well can make disciplining individuals—playing hardball—too emotionally challenging to risk. Without a measure of your own discipline, any one of those fears can be realized, but don't forgo this incredible accelerant over an exaggerated assumption or fear.

Make no mistake about it: leading people is a hard and at times lonely job—but the Wizard of Oz would never have captured the hearts and minds of Dorothy and her followers by hiding behind a curtain. The joys and benefits waiting for you and your team will far outweigh the risks, and you will never cross the barrier to trust without first garnering the loyalty of the individuals on your team.

When you think about fostering growth in the team behind you, the natural inclination is to limit your focus to increasing their faculties, impact, and value for the organization. This is what we're paid to do, after all, and narrowly defining *growth* in that way makes sense for our work. But limiting your perspective to their growth in the current job may not be the most effective move to entice your trailers forward in your draft.

The first step to move an individual from commitment to loyalty is to work your way through the facades to learn your followers' genuine interests and passions—the areas in which *they* want to grow. Once you know their passions, make a concerted effort to engage them.

Every organization has some tasks, assignments, and travel excursions that are sought after, as well as others that people avoid at all costs. The Air Force is no different, and the criteria we used to select individuals for promotions, the best deals, and upgrade training were performance and image. Hard work was certainly a qualifier, but the really good deals went to those who also projected the *image* that they were going to stay with the Air Force for the long haul. To compete in that environment, you had to be good at your job—and convey the *position* that you wanted in the organization's draft in 25 years, even if that was the furthest thing from your mind.

Digging Deeply to Find Genuine Interests

A **position** is an individual's persona, or public face, and it can be expressed in different ways. It may be hard to fathom why some people assume the outward personalities they

> **position**
>
> An individual's persona, or public face; it can be expressed in different ways.

> **passions**
>
> The foundational—the most important—elements in an individual's life that drive his or her actions. Passions are the behind-the-scenes motivators that make individuals' motors run.

do, but the overt intentions of that inspiring go-getter or irritating rabble-rouser may be a front for something he or she feels the need to hide.

Passions on the other hand are the behind-the-scenes motivators that make individuals' motors run. Find people's genuine passions, and you'll find the emotional drivers that will help you lead them to close the gaps between you. The challenge is that followers will reveal their true passions only in low-risk environments—they must feel safe before they'll give them up.*

Although it is not always the case, as a leader what you are likely to get up front is a follower's position, complete with a carefully crafted elevator speech that conveys the sentiment that he or she is with you for the long haul. Trailers will not put their job, promotability, or good deals at risk by revealing their true desires and genuine interests. Cracking that barrier relies entirely on your taking the time to get to know the individuals on your team. People will not give up their personas until they know that you will help them move on

---

*Terry "Mack" McKinney, Concept of Operations (CONOPS) master's course, solidthinking.org, 2008.

their real wants, needs, and passions. And very often those positions are emotionally well defended.

I Was a Follower Once, Too

I can thank one exceptional leader for breaking through my own thick shell to find and then pull on the passion within me. To say he earned my loyalty would be an understatement.

The assignment to Spain was my fourth move with the Air Force. By that point I had developed quite a bit of confidence and had become more outspoken. Mavericks don't fare well in big bureaucracies, and if people were musing about my future, most would have bet I was heading to a life outside the service.

Bruce "Orville" Wright was two grades above me and on a trajectory to become a general officer. We weren't quite opposites, but I never thought he would move on my behalf. Late one afternoon he did just that, by asking if we could talk; I nodded, and he pulled me into a briefing room.

"I've watched you for six months now," he said, "and it's obvious that you work hard in the air and on the ground. You volunteer to fly at every opportunity, and you're one of the most respected fighter pilots in the squadron."

So, what's your point?

"Several folks have started taking an interest in you, and I'm one of them. We think you'd compete well for Junior Officer of the Quarter . . ."

Not interested.

". . . and the wing's only opportunity to send a pilot to back-to-back operational assignments. If we won that, you'd be the only pilot out of the 240 in the wing who gets to fly the F-16 in a combat unit for another three years."

Now I'm listening.

"But I need your help to make it happen. You have the confidence it takes to engage anyone at this base on any issue. Every time you do, a surge of pride runs up *my* spine . . ."

Now you've got me.

". . . but that can be intimidating to others who aren't like-minded. Would you consider letting me carry that ball for you? Engage *me* with the things you believe need changing, and let me take them forward. I've got an ear or two that will listen to me, and you have my word I'll use them. If you'll do that, we just might bring that next assignment home for you. You in?"

Looking back, I was an easy read for anyone willing to take the time to watch me. I wasn't married yet and had no other visible passions beyond flying that jet and being with the people who loved it as much as I did. Orville was the first who took the time to figure me out, and his approach was brilliant.

Moving to overtly further my very real interest in flying fighters was a huge capture tool, but my other interest was at least as powerful, and it would be years before I realized just how ingenious his approach was to mine that hidden jewel.

The persona I fronted with my maverick-like words and actions was actually a passion he could not address directly. Maybe it was because he wasn't sure it was a real interest—or maybe because he wasn't sure *I* knew how much *I* cared for our organization. Either way, his willingness to give my operational concerns a voice was everything I could have asked for. I bought his offer and closed on his wing into loyalty.

Finding Your People's Hidden Passions

While you may believe that the individual posturing in the Air Force is unique to the military, don't be fooled into thinking your people are any different. Many joined your organization for the same reasons they enter the service—to complete their education, get some experience, and build a little capital while they complete plans to move on their real interests.

If you believe in your company and prioritize it above every other aspect of your life, it may be hard for you to see another's logic in wanting something different. That is the very reason why many followers will conceal their passions from you.

To work beyond your own blinders and paradigms, you need a technique for listening and an approach for cracking the shells that protect the pearls in your people's lives.

The Pillars of Life

No matter what kind of people you have behind you—what genders, races, creeds, or nationalities are on your

> **pillars of life**
> Five major areas that individuals can develop in their lives to support their well-being and drive their actions: faith, family, friends, health, and work. Some people have all five pillars at work in their lives; others develop only one or two.

team—everyone has the opportunity to develop five major areas, five **pillars of life** that drive their actions and support their well-being: *faith, family, friends, health,* and *work.* Some folks have all five pillars in their lives, while others choose to develop only one or two.

You need to set aside your own beliefs and priorities for now, as this is not about you; it's about figuring out how to move your people. As you will see in this chapter, the depth of character, the cohesion, and the loyalty of your team members will grow exponentially when you help them move on *their* interests and passions.

Leading People Where They Really Live

Many team leaders make work the central pillar of their lives—and they expect the team behind them to have that same priority. Those who do will elevate an occupation to a high art, and we had more than our fair share of those folks on the Thunderbirds.

Perhaps the most demanding position on the demonstration team was that of our flight-line maintenance supervisor, or line *cone.* The cone managed airframe times, engine overhauls, and every day-to-day operational and inspection aspect you can imagine—all in a job that moved faster than most. On top of all that, the cone was out in front of the jets, directing ground operations for our demonstration.

The job demanded the kind of smarts and time that few folks could muster, and the individual in the job as I came on board had mastered the role. From the jigsaw puzzle of maintenance bookkeeping to the rapport he

developed with our fighter crew chiefs and support personnel, Master Sergeant Donnie McCracken had it down to a
science. I picked up several things about Donnie during my
first two months on the team, but the most important was
that his job appeared to be the biggest pillar in his life.

The passion for the hands-on work of an aircraft maintenance technician is evident in many, and achieving levels
of certification in the field is a cause for real pride. But like
all the other pillars, passion for work can also be evident in
irritating or even disruptive behavior. (Orville Wright might
have said as much about me early in my career!) The secret
is to not zero in on the first things that rise to the surface
but rather to wait until you have a lock on the person's most
precious interests.

Friendship Matters

There are natural linkages among the pillars, and watching
for those relationships allows you to build a more complete
picture of the individuals on your team. Those details
will open doors for engagement, and one of the biggest is
friendship.

The world of a fighter pilot welds two or three of life's
pillars together. The quest to be good in the air requires a
lot of work on the ground, and the time spent after-hours
is fertile ground for friendships. The same people who were
at work in the squadron on Saturday morning had social-
ized together the previous night and would be spotting one
another at the gym that afternoon. The love for the job was
heightened by interlocking friendships in that community,
just like they are in yours.

Friendships provide teammates with the kind of physical and emotional support that comes no other way. Many people have four or five good friends, but only one or two are "firemen." *Firemen* are friends who come running when you call them—no matter what. That kind of friend inside the work environment can be a great barometer and source of insight about your followers. Friends like that further your momentum when things are going well, and they are second only to faith or family when things are going badly.

Faith Matters

Whether or not you are religious, as with every other line of interest this is not about you. It is about the interests of your teammates. Some folks closely guard their religious beliefs, whereas others are very candid about their convictions. They may talk openly about being a church elder or their involvement with church activities, which lets you know that *faith* is a pillar in their lives. It is a sensitive subject in the workplace, and you may find it inappropriate or even against the rules to ask about another's faith, but you will serve your team well if you take the time to *listen for* their beliefs.

What is important to recognize is that faith can be just as significant or irrelevant as the other four pillars in the lives of those behind you. Some of your folks may have come from dysfunctional or broken homes, and they haven't developed the pillar of family. Some may consider themselves loners and won't make the effort to develop friendships. Others give little time or thought to their own health.

Like those individuals, followers who haven't developed the pillar of faith have one less leg to stand on.

Your job in the lead jet is to learn their interests, the pillars that they value, and the pillars that are missing, and then figure out a way to further their momentum while they are on your team.

When you detect an individual's interest, jot down a note or two about what you found. The notes will build a picture of what is driving that person forward—and maybe what's holding him or her back. And by thinking about what you've written, you will enjoy an epiphany or two about how you can further the person's interests. When you move on those epiphanies, you will draw your team-mate closer.

It all starts with a genuine desire to know what makes people tick and then moving on what you hear. Do both, and you'll create the kind of performance, momentum, and unity you need to bring some big brass rings home for your team.

Sometimes It's Not about Work–Even When It Is

Several individuals faced significant life challenges while they were part of the Thunderbirds, but I chose two to give you an idea of the kind of dividends that can be realized on the quest for passions and the want to close the gaps on loyalty. Had we responded to either situation in a bureau-cratic way, both teammates may have lost some wind from their sails, but the team would have lost so much more.

Family Matters

As the Air Force's showcase squadron, the Thunderbirds could not tolerate failures that reflected poorly on the character of the service. Bouncing checks may not be grounds for immediate dismissal, but the repercussions were generally significant, and I was about to engage an otherwise solid performer who had dribbled several. He was almost in tears when he reported in, and his expression intensified as I asked him how someone who had done such great work for the organization could let his finances slip. When I asked why he had failed to take care of his debts, the tears started streaming with the words "It's all my fault, sir."

As he explained, I found out a whole lot more about him and his character. His wife had found a great job downtown and after several months with the additional income, they decided to buy a newer car. A month after the purchase, they found out they were expecting, and at sixth months the pregnancy went high-risk. His wife was put on bed rest, and with that they lost her income. He took two part-time jobs on top of his full-time work with the Thunderbirds to try to cover the car payments, but it wasn't enough.

Pride is a remarkable thing. It will keep some folks driving well beyond what others could stand, just for the right to say they can make it on their own. It will also give the best in your organization a reason to mask their vulnerabilities. No one had known what that man and his family were going through. His performance on the team had not waivered. There had been no change in his demeanor, no fissures in the shield protecting his interests. His work was

an obvious and solid pillar, but the critical passion and challenge in his life at that moment was revealed only by the call
of a creditor.

There was no reason to punish him and every reason
to give him the help he needed to get back on a solid financial
footing. There were several tools available to us to do that,
and we moved as a team to help him recover financially.
What we got in return was one of the most loyal long-ball-
hitting players I knew during my two years on the team.

There are many signs that will let you know whether
family is a key pillar in the life of a teammate. Photos on
desks, conversations about Little League, in-law visits and
the like—all open windows of opportunity for you to assess
the importance of family in a team member's life.

Remembering names and birthdates, sporting activities and accomplishments, and special needs and illnesses
of team members' families will give you openings to engage
them on a personal level. And if you make a habit of check-
ing in with a targeted question about their families, you will
get them to lean in to you.

Loyalty is won through small acts that further the
interests of the people around you. By limiting your conversation to their professional presence and progression, you
miss not only the chance to bring another into the lane of
loyalty but also all-too-scarce opportunities to bind your
team together.

Health Matters

Cheryl Allen was very open about being a nine-year cancer
survivor when she stepped into the Thunderbird hangar.
She breezed through the first 20 days of our onboarding

program, but word came that she might falter under the pressure of the twenty-first day. Many folks reeled during that final ceremony as they answered my questions while surrounded by the whole team.

Cheryl, however, was so nervous that she all but forgot her name as she reported in. The opening question was meant to be a confidence builder, but she received it like a knockout blow. Her knees buckled, and just when I thought she was heading for the floor, somehow she pulled it together. She answered that question and all of those that followed, with an ever-growing wave of confidence. The hangar exploded in applause the moment I stapled our patch on her uniform. It was a surge in momentum, a moment I will never forget.

And then life intervened. Several months later Cheryl's pillar of health all but crumbled when she suffered a cancer recurrence. In light of her recent patching ceremony, the diagnosis hit our team pretty hard. The surgery would be immediate, and her recovery would rely on every other pillar she had developed in her life.

I had no notions about Cheryl's faith, but she was new to the base and almost all of her friends were on our team. Both of her parents had already passed, and her siblings lived hundreds of miles away. The support that normally came from family and friends would all have to come from the Thunderbirds. Our team now had the opportunity to help shore up and strengthen our teammate and see her through this storm.

The military is a funny place. It is filled with people who willingly fight to the death alongside or for another, but we are not supposed to get sick. When someone's life is threatened by disease in that environment, many become so locked up over what to say or do that they don't do anything. To give Cheryl our support, we would have to get past that baffle. One of our supervisors, Master Sergeant Mike Noska, and I discussed the possibilities, and we kept coming back to Cheryl's indelible patching ceremony. The patching ritual, and the patch itself, meant a great deal to all of us. With just a little imagination, we could use it to get the entire team to cast their lots for her.

Two hours after our talk, Mike walked back into my office with the epiphany that was born out of our conversation. He had taken one of our big unit decals, glued it to a piece of wood, and cut it into a 130-piece jigsaw puzzle. We called the entire team together and asked each to take a piece of that puzzle, write their name and a word or two of encouragement on the back, and then take it to Cheryl in the hospital. If all they could say was "We miss you" before they departed, it would have a huge impact. It worked better than we could have imagined. You could see Cheryl's color change as every piece of that puzzle was assembled next to her, and you could feel the connective tissue among us grow.

I am sure Cheryl would have gotten by without our involvement, but can you imagine having a more furthering wind at your back? Reaching out to one of our own who was in genuine need reinforced an already special bond. And the impact, the surge in emotion within the team, was huge.

With just a little thought, you can find an opportunity to connect with every member of *your* team. Although you will not find directions for developing that kind of loyalty in your job description, don't miss the opportunity to foster it. It will move your people and fuel the kind of growth that will affect every facet of your working world. It makes people want to close ranks, run faster, and spin ever tighter together. And it can make your organization the one your members point to as the best of the lot when they look back at the end of their working lives.

How Passions Close the Gaps on Our Goals

Meeting the wants and needs of your people not only is a good thing to do but it will also further your team's drive to capture your organizational goals. Remember the Thunderbirds' goal to increase our audience and build up our brand? Really tapping the passions of our people and securing their loyalty is what helped us get there.

The hurdles to live-stream a video feed of our flights were bigger than you might think. During our discussions it became obvious that our maintenance officer, Hawk Hawkins, thrived on the kind of political challenges others would have balked at. Streaming live airshows had at least as many regulatory and organizational challenges as it did technical obstacles. Those barriers would have caused many to recommend that we scuttle the effort, but Hawk lived for those types of challenges. Giving him free rein to obtain the technical approvals and equipment we needed to make it happen would pull him forward in our draft.

Answering Desire with Hope

Our support for the Make-A-Wish Foundation was a major part of our public outreach, and we needed someone to lead that effort. My left wingman, Chase Boutwell, loved kids, and in my mind he needed no more incentive than the mere opportunity to increase our impact on Make-A-Wish families, but there was an opportunity to pull him even farther forward.

We had hired four demonstration pilots the year he came on board, and Chase was hired for just one year to bring our hiring cadence back to three demo pilots per training season. Keeping him for three years would accomplish the same goal, and while there was an opportunity to do that, there were some very good reasons not to. Our travel schedule put a burden on every team member's family, but the demonstration pilots were the only ones who deployed on every trip—and they did it for two straight years. That tempo tested the best of families.

After watching Chase throughout training season, I broached the subject of his one-year tenure and asked if he would be interested in staying longer. Just the thought lit him up. I could not guarantee anything, but if he showed the tenacity to run that distance with style, I would do everything I could to make it happen. He left my office beaming, and I knew his efforts to further the momentum of our Make-A-Wish program would be that much more intense.

What your followers value is important, and helping them attain what they need to flourish is one of the most gratifying aspects of leadership. Every person in your draft has at least one pillar that means more than the others. With just a little effort, you can motivate your trailers with the kind of momentum that makes them carriers of loyalty— and they will in turn foster it in the folks in *their* draft. Once you find and nurture their passions, your job is to keep them moving forward by giving them your confidence.

CHAPTER 6

Close the Confidence Gap

Confidence is your faith in people—in their leadership, faculties, and judgment. It is one of the most vital elements of drafting and is easy to overlook. No matter how long individuals have been in your profession, each has developed skills through considerable time and effort, and most will do their best to further the team's goals. But along the way, many develop doubts about their impact or will wonder if the folks around them actually value what they do. Their self-esteem is a critical enabler of your team's momentum, and you can grow that by openly valuing their efforts, talents, and professional competencies. Whether you do that one-on-one or in a group setting—formally and informally—reinforcing your confidence in your people will help you close a critical gap in your draft.

> **confidence**
> One's faith in people—in their leadership, faculties, and judgment.

I remember how one commander showed confidence in the new guy—and it stands out in my memory because

that new guy was me. I had just joined our wing as it was
beginning its annual bomb-dropping competition, or turkey
shoot. Our wing weapons officer tabulated the scores as
his last act before he moved on to his next assignment, and
my job was to take his seat in the organization. The awards
ceremony at the officers' club was conducted with no small
amount of fanfare, as Top Guns and the Top Squadron were
announced and celebrated. These awards could really make
a career.

I didn't fly in the competition, but I was certainly
interested in the results. When the raw scores were posted,
something didn't look right. I took the numbers home and
recalculated them several times, and every tally reinforced
my fears: the awards for our biggest annual competition had
gone to the wrong individuals and the wrong squadron.

Colonel John Barry commanded our operations
group. Being a new guy, I didn't know him from Adam.
I was about to bring him bad news, and my experience
with senior leaders responding to any form of it to that
point had been, well, disappointing. After thinking through
the options and likely outcomes, I moved to engage
Colonel Barry.

When I finished explaining what I found, he thanked
me, asked a few questions for clarity, and then asked how
I thought we should remedy the situation. Outwardly,
I remained stoic through a pause that lasted maybe only a
second, but my mind was racing. He didn't blame me. He
didn't ask how many others knew or if we could just let
this little embarrassment go. He asked how I thought we
should fix it.

I suggested that we admit our mistake, let those who had received trophies keep them, and reissue the awards at a smaller ceremony one Friday in the near future.

"Great idea," he said. "We need to fix this just as soon as we can. Let me know when you have the new trophies ready, and we'll make it happen."

We often think about deference in terms of what we owe those above us in the chain, but Colonel Barry showed me that respect goes both ways. The first side of that equation is reinforcing your belief in the people who follow you, by giving them your respect and your confidence.

Resisting the Temptation to Withhold Your Confidence

If you started in business as a structural engineer and over time built your own construction company, the opportunity and maybe the desire to dictate or second-guess the actions of your team's structural engineers will always be there. Oversight is certainly your job, but the chores of running your company likely mean that you are no longer keeping up with the profession. Technology, techniques, and building codes change frequently enough that you would miss something your experts would not. Even many of the habits and crosschecks associated with doing the job every day will very likely become rusty over time.

When you forgo or override the judgment of those behind you over a preference or due to pride, the effects on your draft are predictable. The value of displaying confidence in your followers may not seem important unless you think back on the times when you were not given the credibility you thought you deserved. There have been many leaders over the course of my working life who, like Colonel Barry, propelled me forward with their confidence. But there were others who let their pride dominate in ways that would literally take my breath away. One such moment in Spain compromised much more than my confidence.

Undermining by Overcontrolling

It was one of those days when the entire Iberian Peninsula was shrouded with clouds from the ground up to 8,000 feet. To complicate things the part of Spain we would be flying over had no navigational aids that were available to us. To stay in the area, we would rely entirely on our inertial navigation systems (INSs), which worked well most of the time.

The upgrading (student) pilot was flying in the lead aircraft, and I would be both his wingman and the instructor of record for the mission. Our squadron commander was flying the number 3 jet, and we had a relatively inexperienced pilot flying as number 4. By the time we got to the end of the runway, number 4 was showing a ground speed of 50 miles per hour when he was right next to us. It was a clear sign that his INS was failing. These were the days before global positioning systems (GPSs), and taking him airborne would have put him at risk. We could easily complete the sortie with three aircraft, so I directed him to ground-abort and taxi back to the chalks.

Our squadron commander chimed in and asked again about his ground speed. When number 4 told him it was now 75 miles per hour, our commander did the unthinkable: he overrode my direction and told number 4 to fly the mission as planned.

The working area was just like the weather forecast had predicted: we could not see anything on the ground. The plan called for number 4 to hold in the northern part of the airspace while the other three proceeded south for 10 minutes of work. Number 4's INS would have been drifting at well over 100 miles per hour by this point in the mission, which meant he was holding over an imaginary point that was moving across the ground at that same speed.

When we completed maneuvering in the south, we turned to run an intercept on number 4, but he was nowhere to be found. We had no idea which direction his INS was taking him. After looking for 15 minutes, numbers 1 and 2 were running on fumes and were forced to head home.

Through something of a miracle, our squadron commander managed to find number 4 and bring him home. During the debrief I asked him why he had overridden my decision to leave number 4 on the ground. His response put a nail in the coffin of loyalty: "There was *no problem*, WAS THERE, JV?"

Keeping people off balance is certainly a method of control, but it can poison their desire to follow—and their ability to lead. Showing the folks behind us that we value their judgment, technical skills, and willingness to extend themselves for the organization gives them our confidence and accelerates their momentum.

Empowering Confidence on the Thunderbirds

Sustaining the integrity and professionalism within our demonstration was critical. The individual in charge of that operation was as organized and as driven as they come. Just watching Lieutenant Colonel Mike "Slam" Byrne, my operations officer, was something special. Slam also acted as the safety officer for our demonstrations, and he graded every performance. His eye for perfection in our maneuvering was unbelievably keen, and his people skills were among the best I have ever known. Both were on display during our mission debriefs.

There were countless days when he caught the smallest formation errors or would call out a pilot for being 10 feet below a 150-foot target altitude when that jet was still 2 miles away. His skill was matched only by his ability to convey the point in a way that made the offending pilot acknowledge the mistake and, more often than not, smile in the process. Closing the confidence gap with Slam meant standing behind his judgment, and the best way I could do that was in my response to his critiques of *my* performance during those sessions.

The opportunities to give your confidence are everywhere and can often be delivered in the form a simple question. Remember our audacious goal to double our numbers? At the end of many days, our public affairs officer, Guy Hunneyman, would walk into my office and ask for a few minutes of my time. On other days he stormed in with the words "Mentor me!" His public affairs staff was still not buying in on our brand awareness initiative and continued to sustain their rationale for not moving on the cereal box or any other ideas we gave them. We talked about approaches to each of his team's objections—about funding, priorities, and Guy's own doubts about our objective to double the team's exposure. As frustrated as he must have been, he wasn't ready to give up.

Late one evening I told him he had every skill he needed to lead his team, but I knew he must be getting worn down and asked if he wanted me to engage his staff directly. I could not help smiling when he took offense at my suggestion. He walked out that night more determined than ever.

A few days later, he came in, wanting something more than a conversation. He wanted a concession, a device, a tool he could use to attract the kind of attention that would double our numbers. "Air Force public affairs is for it, and I have tentative dates for interviews with *20/20* and *Dateline NBC*. We can make every milestone you have given us happen if you'll talk about your beating cancer." His team didn't just come together to help craft a plan, they had run the traps to see if it was feasible. I agreed with every suggestion his team offered—and just like that our biggest goal had momentum.

Bolstering the value and respect you hold for your people can be very involved or as simple as saying, "Let's just wait and see how this plays out." Either way you will gain much more than a follower by standing behind them—even when you don't know them very well.

Letting Things Play Out

John Bartrum had been with the National Institutes of Health (NIH) for only a few weeks, but as the budget director he still could not believe what he was hearing.

His organization had accepted money from Congress to execute a program, but several of its key internal leaders were backing away from their commitment due to unforeseen labor challenges. To top it off, they were insisting on keeping the earmarked funds to pay for other things.

Bartrum issued a memo acknowledging the personnel challenges and then he made two distinct requests. The first directed the teams (institutes and centers) that could handle more grants to identify themselves. The second directed those who could sustain their commitments to reaffirm their support. Once his office had the inputs, he would shift the funding from those that could not execute the tasks Congress had given them to those that could. Confirmation was due by the end of the following business day.

Several institute and center leaders caused an uproar and decided to go over Bartrum's head; they petitioned the director of the NIH to kill the memo.

The NIH director, Dr. Elias A. Zerhouni, knew that pulling the memo would relieve the tension that was now consuming much of his organization. But Bartrum was not only right, he had extended himself—he had put himself at risk to sustain the integrity of the organization. If Dr. Zerhouni pulled the memo, he would disembowel Bartrum's effectiveness as a leader for the rest of his tenure at the NIH. The director's response was perfect: "The memo said, 'by the end of the day,' and we can wait until 5 p.m." With those simple words, he gave Bartrum all the support he could ask for—time for the memo to take effect. By five o'clock that afternoon, all 27 suborganizations within the NIH had revalidated their commitments. Did the director's confidence earn Bartram's loyalty? You bet it did.

Giving your followers your backing is critical to cultivating their loyalty, but that is just one of several aspects of confidence that you can offer the trailers in your draft. Another, very effective method is developing a recurring recognition program.

Recognizing Your Best

The traditions and rituals on the Thunderbirds served several purposes. Most, like our weekly predeparture briefings, were designed to realign, energize, and spin the organization up for one of our 40 annual deployments. But there were two rituals whose sole purpose was to focus the organization's energies on elevating the individuals on the team. Each was designed to deliver recognition, and both were unique. One provided regular, informal recognition, and the other delivered formal recognition through a single award at the end of every show season.

Delivering Informal Recognition

Juan Williams was one incredible teammate. It wasn't just the big things he did for the Thunderbirds that accelerated the team around him. He made a habit of showing up early each morning during training season to make sure his peers' transition from the end of one long workday into the next was a little easier. By 4:30 on any morning, the other crew chiefs and assistants would show up to the flight line and find their heavy tool boxes wheeled out in place, the canopies open, and the aircraft forms next to each of their F-16s. Selfless efforts like Juan's invigorated a collective will to answer in kind, and every time we turned around

someone was giving a little more of him- or herself to
further the efforts of the whole.

I wasn't the only one who took notice, but I did. I kept
track of as many such things as I could on the cards I crafted
to memorize names as I came on board the team. When
the opportunity to brag about one of our players presented
itself, I would pull out the card and put those notes to use.
Fortunately, someone long before me had created those
opportunities with something we called a *FARKLE,* an event
(and weighty acronym) comprising *friends and relatives,
kin,* [and] *likely extensions.*

Our 130 Thunderbirds were from all over the United
States, and over the course of a year we would fly shows
near many of their hometowns. When those two beams
crossed, it provided an opportunity to recognize team
members in a very special way. We would invite up to 50 of
the folks who were closest to our targeted teammate to join
us on the field the day of the airshow.

When they arrived we would load them up in a bus
and take them out to one of our beautiful jets. As they
stepped out of the bus, every officer on the team would
greet them. We would take some keepsake photographs and
then surround the group for a little show-and-tell. I would
tell them a little about our team and the role *their* Thunderbird had in making the demonstration happen.

It was all designed to make those closest to our teammate realize how much we valued their loved one. The
things that moved the families were never accomplishments
you would find in the official record; it was the little things
they did that allowed us to run faster and spin tighter as
an organization that evoked the tears of pride. And when

we moved Mom and Dad that way, I was reaching into the chest of our Thunderbird to pull him or her a little closer.

The remarkable thing about FARKLEs was how little they cost and how big a dividend they delivered. The VIP passes were given to us by show sites, and with a team photographer on hand the only real cost came down to time. And in the end, time and your genuine presence are the greatest gifts you can give your people, and that combination paid off big for our draft.

Informal recognition on *your* team No matter what you do or where you are within your organizational structure, a program like FARKLE can have an immense impact. There are many different ways you can design it, but remember three things as you do: keep it simple, be sincere, and stay present. Any recurring program must be simple, inexpensive, and easy to execute if it's going to be perpetuated, so keep it that way. Put a positional leader, like your executive assistant, in charge of setting it up; then all you have to do is brag.

If you really don't know what your honoree has done, your effort will miss the mark, so start by taking time to notice the little things your people do. It is okay to use notes in these gatherings, but your words must come from the heart. This last thought has a bit of an edge to it: Before you start bragging, make sure a majority of your team is surrounding the honoree and the folks he or she is closest to. The presence of peers will bring its own energy to your target of interest—and your words will make the teammates think about what *they* want you to be able to say about *them* when they are in the center of that circle.

The number of ideas and the opportunities for you to recognize your people are limitless, and very often the simplest things can mean the most to your people. A man named Art Rooney used that thought to build the kind of cohesion every team should strive for.

Writing the book on loyalty   Everyone with the Pittsburgh Steelers, from the biggest star athlete to the newest member of the grounds crew, seemed to feel a special bond with Art Rooney. For whatever reason, they all knew he had their best interests at heart. He was a prolific writer, and a handwritten card from him was a treasure.

What was often unusual about those cards were the recipients. Rooney wrote one card after he had traded Steelers running back Greg Hawthorne to another team. The card went to Hawthorne's new coach and simply read, "I got to know the young man. He's a fine human being who can contribute to the success of any team." The relationship between Rooney and Hawthorne was so close that when his new coach showed him the card, it brought tears to Hawthorne's eyes.

Tony Dungy played with the team for two years in the late 1970s. When Dungy left the Steelers, Rooney wrote a similar note to his parents. Both notes were about people who had already left the team, but the trickle-down effect was huge. Those two men picked up the phone and told their former Steelers teammates what the old man had done; when they realized that his loyalty didn't end with their time on the Steelers, the impact of his cards snowballed. It wasn't the big-ticket items that generated loyalty on that team; the lifelong loyalty Rooney fostered with his people came at the cost of a postcard.*

If you take the time to get to know the individuals on your team, spend another moment or two to build a plan to capture them. When you learn the nuances of their lives, the epiphanies will come for how you can genuinely touch them in ways that cost next to nothing. Recognizing your people in even a small way will bolster their confidence and gain you their loyalty.

Delivering Formal Recognition

The Fitzgerald Award was presented annually to the Thunderbird who had contributed the most to the team's mission during the previous 12 months. The winner was selected by secret ballot, and anyone from a show-line crew chief to an administrative specialist could win the trophy.

Kevin Gruenwald, one of the team photographers, was selected the year I joined the team. His work with a camera made him a standout on the ground and in the air, but even when he was not behind the lens he seemed to be everywhere, helping every lane within the team. The same was true of Mike Noska, our sortie support superintendent, who won it the following year, and Shaun Hardwick, my incredible crew chief, who won it the next. I would love to say that I influenced their selection, but I didn't. My engagement with the selection process would have diluted the value of the award on many levels.

---

*Ron Cook, "The Chief: Art Rooney Sr.—A Decade after His Death Still, Pittsburgh's No. 1 Citizen," post-gazette.com, 30 August 1998.

Formal recognition on *your* team   Setting up a formal recognition program is easy, so long as you build in value early and respect its purity. As with all things, lineage will give the award its foundational value. Name it after someone the team knows and respects as a hard worker or an influential individual. The Fitzgerald Award was named after the commander/leader who started the Airman of the Year Award in 1960 and who was killed in a crash the following year. That is lineage.

When your teammates embrace the value of the award and are given responsibility for sustaining that value, they will take their individual ballots seriously. Give this task to one of your most trusted people to administer and keep your own hand away from the ballot box. *Your* job should be limited to finding the funds it takes to make the award a heavy one to carry off the stage and to presenting it with all the pomp and circumstance your best deserve. Whatever token, trophy, or plaque you come up with, it must be as special as the individual after whom it is named. The bronze replica mounted on top of the "Fitz" trophy, coupled with its emotional worth, made it a treasure for life.

Once you have closed the confidence gap, the folks behind you will feel the surge within and be left with the want to move further forward in your draft. What they find when they get there will depend largely on how you develop their respect for you.

CHAPTER 7

Close the Respect Gap

The toughest moments during your tenure will be even more challenging when you lead your team in a different direction from the one they had in mind. The heat your actions generate during those engagements will be significant, and no one will feel the rise in temperature more than you do. But you must be willing to set aside your popularity and use your authority to bolster the team's performance.

> **respect**
> A feeling of admiration or high regard for the qualities of another.

You will be moving against the grain, but there are times when you have to make that choice. As much as some would like to believe otherwise, your team's willingness to follow you relies on the *respect* they have for you—how highly you are held in their esteem. Developing that respect must be a conscious act, and when you do it right, you will pull your followers forward in your draft, right up to the threshold of trust.

I had the opportunity to make many interesting calls during my tenure on the point of the Thunderbirds, but one really hit home. I had championed the effort to get the team's first Air Force recruiter to join our ranks, and the man I selected was stumbling badly.

The Saga of William Smiley

It was the eleventh day of Sergeant William Smiley's training, and something was not right. The Thunderbird onboarding (patching) program was run by a board of senior non-commissioned officers (NCOs), and they asked to see me. The ranking member opened up with a jaw dropper: Sergeant Smiley had to go. He had become flippant about the chores and memorization requirements of the program and had failed the first oral exam. It was hard not to take the final line personally: "We know he's *your* guy—that you handpicked him to be the first Thunderbird recruiter—but he's not a good fit, and we'd like your support for his removal from the team."

I openly revisited several examples they gave and their rationale for removing Sergeant Smiley from the team. I voiced several things that were troubling me: about my in-brief with Sergeant Smiley and my own concerns with his record as an independent recruiter—they are by definition "lone wolves"—and we had thrown him into one of the most intensive team immersion programs imaginable. How could we be surprised that he had failed?

I thanked each of them for having the courage to engage me directly, adding that I believed in our standards and that compromising the onboarding program was out of the question. But I needed time for coordination and to think through the options before I made a decision. They

filed out of my office without a word, but the pall of disappointment they left behind was thick.

Being Willing to Go against the Grain

Going against the advice or wishes of your team generates
the kind of turbulence and organizational heat that causes
many leaders to forgo the opportunity and simply go along
with the group. Seeking the advice and counsel of those
around you can be a good thing, but abdicating your judgment and authority to them is completely different.

No one knows your team or the challenges you're
facing better than you do. Teams thrive with leaders who
pick up their authority like a baseball bat and swing for the
fence, not those who sit back and hope the pitcher named
Fate misses the plate four times and gives them a free pass
to the next base. A safe "base-on-balls" mentality may
curry the favor of your followers, and it may even get you
promoted, but organizations don't accelerate with that kind
of leadership, and no one respects the leaders who adopt it.
What prevents people from using their authority to lead?

Having authority gives you the right to lead, but it
doesn't guarantee that you will *use* your authority or that
people will follow. **Authority** is the power to give orders,
make decisions, and direct or control someone or something. Most of us are given the
reins to lead our teams through
legal and positional authorities
that come from society or our
parent organizations. There is
another kind of authority that is

> **authority**
> The power to give
> orders, make decisions,
> and direct or control
> someone or something.

different in that a leader's gifts, talents, and personality are special enough to make others *want* to defer their decisions, opinions, or direction to their leader: *charismatic* authority.

Getting people to follow a change of course can test the best of us. Even military leaders, with all of our legal and positional trappings, face the same challenge of getting folks to move in a new direction. To be successful you've got to be willing to use the authority you've been granted.

Whether running a prison at the height of the Roman Empire or leading your own business here and now, the drive for success can give you the courage it takes to use your authority and lead your team, but it's not the only incentive. Success can be a powerful carrot, but your fears can play as big a role in driving you forward.

Was His Only Tool a Hammer?

Our fighter wing had failed a major operational readiness inspection, and the leadership above the wing took quick action to fix the problem. They fired our wing commander, replaced him with a leader known throughout the Air Force as a "fixer," and then set an aggressive timetable for our reevaluation.

We knew we were in trouble the moment Colonel Mike "Conan" Barbien set foot on our base. In his mind whatever we had been doing had not worked, and he quickly made it obvious he wasn't going to take any real input from his new leadership team. That was hard to swallow when every operational, maintenance, and support unit in the wing had received an excellent or outstanding grade during our failed evaluation. It was only the most senior leadership that was cited for our overall failing grade.

Conan seemed to thrive on being unpredictable even when we flew with him. We never knew when we would be berated for not giving him the most basic instruction befitting a new pilot, or for briefing him with less respect than is due to one with his vast flying experience. Some would say he kept us on our toes, but he really just kept us all off balance.

In the year that preceded our failed evaluation, we deployed three times to a forward operating base for seven weeks at a shot to exercise our wartime roles. As tired and demoralized as we were, we had to start that schedule all over again, and the only thing Conan seemed to care about was passing our looming evaluation.

You might be able to predict how the wing performed in its evaluation—and Conan's success—but let's set aside his end-game achievements for a moment and sort through his potential drivers and motivations. He obviously had the authority to lead, and his style was blunt-force trauma. What could possibly drive an individual to take such an approach with any organization?

Which Brass Ring for You: Popularity or Success?

The two biggest accolades you can receive as a team leader are popularity and success. Unfortunately, most of us are driven more by our fears than by the promise of accolades. The two greatest fears for most leaders on point are the fear of failure and the loss of popularity within the team. Few people willingly accept the stigma associated with failure, and it is hard to fathom anyone actually *wanting* to be unpopular. The question becomes which of the two holds the greatest leverage on you—is it the loss of popularity or a fear of failure? The answer may not be readily apparent, but it can be detected through your style and willingness to use your authority to move those behind you.

Just about any style of leadership can be effective so long as it is balanced and the leader's primary focus is on performance. The graph Popularity or Success depicts the likely impact of a leader's balancing those two driving fears—loss of popularity and failure—on organizational performance. The vertical axis depicts the performance of any team, and the horizontal axis depicts (in the extreme) units led by individuals driven by popularity on the left and by fear of failure on the right (see Popularity or Success).

Popularity or Success: *A Leader's Motivation Affects Team Performance*

Any organization can function and deliver some level of service without credible leadership. You can call the individual on the left side of the scale a pushover, cheerleader, pawn, or figurehead, but, for whatever reason, that person sits in a position of authority that he or she will not use. Leaders at this extreme are placeholders. They keep their chairs from flying up and striking innocent bystanders, but they aren't likely to inspire the performance of, or take disciplinary action on, their people.

On the far right are leaders who are so driven to succeed they are willing to figuratively crush those who fail to measure up. Call these leaders tyrants, dictators, autocrats, or drug lords, but you get the picture. As onerous as they are, these folks are typically more successful than those at the other extreme because of their willingness to use their authority.

Although it is interesting to speculate about where different leaders in our lives fit on the continuum, it is much more effective to look at the curve from inside the mind of a single leader.

It doesn't matter whether you view yourself as a pushover or a tyrant; there is a center point, a place that lies between the extremes, where you live and lead day by day. Put yourself in the center of this graph and think about the positions to the left and right of you.

If you strive to make the work environment enjoyable for your people, at what point are you willing to put your popularity at risk to improve your team's performance? If you see yourself as a nail driver, when are you willing to back off your drive for perfection to build morale and retention into your team? No matter where your comfort zone lies, you must be willing to move off that center to maximize your team's performance.

The Lefts and Rights of the Smiley Dilemma

As soon as the 21-day program's leadership cleared my office, I telephoned the recruiting service colonel who had been so helpful in getting William Smiley into our unit and told her about my predicament. She offered three replacement candidates on the spot. It would take several months to happen, but if I decided to relieve Sergeant Smiley, we would still get a recruiter in the hangar, which was my first consideration.

Relieving that young recruiter could actually bolster the internal value—the morale—of our team. It would reinforce our standards and all team members' innate belief that they were part of a select group. Giving Sergeant Smiley another shot at our squadron patch, on the other hand, could take us in the opposite direction. If the situation were not handled correctly, it would be seen as a compromise of the team's standards to capture a now *political* goal a little more quickly.

I was more concerned with improving the team's performance than with upsetting the apple cart, and I had to fully consider the option of giving Sergeant Smiley a second chance. If he were somehow able turn the situation around, as unlikely as that might be, it could potentially save us months in getting the initiative off the ground.

Completely disregarding the recommendations of the NCOs who ran our onboarding program would be a mistake. I could visualize what the erosion in confidence would do to their place in my draft. Their slide back away from me would be subtle, but the expanding gap would slow the team's momentum. They were concerned about our standards, and I had to do more than just validate those concerns.

The next morning I met again with the NCOs and told them I would engage Sergeant Smiley that afternoon and make a final assessment based on his response. In my mind he probably wouldn't survive the meeting, but, *if* he did and *if* I gave him a reprieve, *we* would give him a legitimate shot—a second chance at making the team. If I reinstated Sergeant Smiley, he would have to start the onboarding program over from day one, and if he proved worthy of a squadron patch, he would get one. But if he fell short, there was no need to come back into my office—the board's judgment would be final. They acknowledged my direction and then left in miffed silence.

That afternoon Sergeant Smiley reported to my office. Talking loudly enough to really get his attention—and to be heard by those who may be eavesdropping—I told him he had disregarded my in-brief at his own peril. He had made no attempt to integrate himself into the organization— hadn't lifted a finger to try to assimilate into his new team. He had also let his own recruiting service down, a recruiting service that was so aggravated by his actions that it had already coordinated his replacement. "I'm ready to relieve you right now. Do you have anything to say?"

His bluster fell away, and the tears began to flow. "I want another chance."

I continued projecting through him with my conditions. *If* he were reinstated, he would start the 21-day program all over again—start it as if he had never set foot in the hangar, except he had already turned the entire team against him. He would have to reengage every one of them and try to turn the tide of emotions he had caused. If he fell short, there would be no further meetings between us. He would be removed from the squadron immediately and sent back to the recruiting service. "Knowing how badly you have stacked the deck against yourself, do you really want to start all over again?"

He looked me in the eye and said, "Yes, sir, I do."

As he left my office, I had no idea how either one of us would fare with this second chance. If he failed, the repercussions for both of us would be significant. But if he could somehow pull it off, we would do much more than save the six months it would take to get his replacement.

We'll return to Sergeant Smiley's story in a moment. For now, know that going against the grain, against the advice or wishes of your team, has risks, but you will inevitably be confronted with that choice. You can either embrace your place at the wheel, and the isolation inherent with leading a team, or you can avoid making waves by floating with the current. I have watched several leaders move with some effect in both extremes, but each option has risks, and one colleague's quest for popularity may shed some light on the associated perils.

They'll Never Turn on a Friend, or Will They?

Bill "Rook" Knight had been in charge of his organization for more than a year. Social by nature, he was both friendly and familiar with everyone in the unit. He relied on the warmth and goodwill he had built with his team to make things happen, and he enjoyed a level of popularity that few leaders experience. Rook was one of the boys right up until fate caught up with him, and fate is a hunter.

A mishap occurred in front of several spectators, and word of the accident's severity rapidly got back to Rook's boss. Although no one was injured and property damage was relatively insignificant, it was only luck that kept the incident from being an all-out catastrophe. The investigation that followed confirmed procedural failures, and Rook's boss elected to override his protective efforts and directed him to relieve one of the men involved in the accident.

Rook reluctantly relieved his friend, but he let it be known that it was not his idea and that he didn't support the move. It could have been his inability to protect his teammate or his attempt to distance himself from such a harsh action that tripped the wire, but with it he lost his charismatic authority. When he failed to support the leaders who gave him his positional authority, he was dead in the water.

Meetings that had once been frank but respectful turned into shouting matches. I watched in disbelief as one subordinate left his chair in the middle of a tirade, walked right up to Rook, and said, "If you *ever* do that again, I will [*expletive*] *kill you!*" The weight of leadership Rook had avoided by riding with the whims of the team was now upon him, and his response was retreat. Whatever admiration the men and women had had for him was gone—he had lost their respect. Rook could have prevented it all if he had been willing to set an *edge.*

The Edge

An *edge* is an attitude, a tone, an expectation of account-ability that compels your team to act on your authority and follow your lead. Many leaders think of themselves as co-directors of a movement and lead their teams more or less as peers. They equate an edge with creating an environment of intimidation, coercion, and fear, and shouldn't we be well above that?

> **edge**
>
> An attitude, a tone, an expectation of accountability that compels your team to act on your authority and follow your lead.

While there is certainly good reason to avoid the extremes, be careful not to be swayed by the notion that anything that compels another to act on your direction is wrong. Even *charisma* is defined as the "compelling" attractiveness or charm that can inspire devotion in others. Folks revel in warmth when they please a charismatic leader, and warmth can be a huge unifier. But the fear of falling out of favor with a charismatic leader can be a powerful driver, and that can create an effective edge.

You have been around leaders with an edge your entire life. Think back to when you were a member of a sports team going through preseason training. If you disappointed your coach, he or she very likely reshaped your drive, technique, or willingness to listen by having you run extra laps or knock out a few extra pushups. Meet or exceed that coach's expectations, and you avoided the extra laps and occasionally were rewarded with praise or a position of leadership on the squad.

Whatever method of praise they offer or punishment they inflict, good coaches embed the belief that you will receive a warm and fuzzy sensation for doing well and a cold and prickly one for not giving your all. The edge is established when your team knows where the extremes of praise and punishment lie—and when they have confidence that you'll hold the line in between.

The point is that you are who you are, and your style has led you to the successes you've achieved in life. But if it hasn't happened already, life on the point will test your mettle. When those moments arise, your team has to *know* that you value success over popularity.

Establishing Your Edge

No matter where you are on the pushover/tyrant spectrum, two rules of thumb apply: The first is start off a little harder, a little farther right of wherever you think your center point might be. The second is have a plan to move back to *your* center when it catches.

When you move to take over a new team or you move up within one you've been on for a while, your people need to know that you value success over popularity. We may not have liked him very much, but Conan the hard-nosed wing commander led our team to a successful reevaluation. No matter what your style of leadership, start off firm, a little to the right of your own center. For some that may mean smiling or talking less frequently. For others it may mean letting your question sit, without trying to minimize the uncomfortable silence by explaining it away or by offering options from which your team may choose (see Establish Your Edge).

Establish Your Edge: *Start Right of Your Own Center*

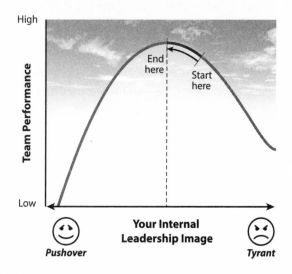

When you start off hard, you always have the option to lighten up, but starting off easy will make turning up the heat a challenge and will put your people off balance while they get used to the new environment. Rook Knight was a good man in a tough predicament, but don't think you are any less susceptible to the siren's song of popularity or that you can turn up the heat when you need to.

Whatever technique you use, set your edge at the start of your tenure and hold it until your team catches. Whether you are leading a sales team, a nonprofit named Benevolence, or a class of third-graders, to lead effectively you need to set an edge.

An edge will minimize whining and unfiltered complaints. It will cause people to prepare more before they step into your office and to think through solutions to problems before they seek your counsel. And it will build and reinforce their respect for you in ways you might not be able to predict.

The Verdict of the 21-Day Jury

It had been 20 days since the NCOs had told me that "my" recruiter, William Smiley, needed to go, and as the indoctrination board piled back into my office, I could smell the crow cooking. The spokesperson for the board looked solemn, almost hurt as he spoke. Not one of them had agreed with my decision to reinstate Sergeant Smiley. They felt I was making a mistake, but they did as they were directed and gave him a second shot. Incredibly, Sergeant Smiley had done a 180. He managed to win over the entire squadron, one person at a time. The NCOs were proud of his efforts and felt that he would be a great addition to the team and had earned the right to wear our squadron patch. The spokesperson wanted me to know one more thing: they were grateful that I was willing to take a risk on the man and entrust them to see it through.

The next day Sergeant Smiley met me on the hangar floor, surrounded by every member of our team, and I choked up as he boldly stepped into my every question. His onboarding almost didn't happen, but when it did it put wind in our sails and, if only for a moment, elevated our crew to an even higher plane.

Having a Plan for When It Catches

The weight associated with any leadership role comes from a variety of directions. Establishing an edge will make you feel the personal side of that weight as soon as you take over your team, which is a reason why some leaders choose to forgo it. One of the great things about an edge is that once it takes hold, you can begin to shift that weight onto others in a way that elevates both their respect for you and their respect for themselves.

The Thunderbird 21-day program was run by a team of NCOs. The weight, the edge, of our onboarding was entirely in their hands. During my two years in command of that team, the situation with Sergeant Smiley was the only instance in which I felt the need to step in, to come off my center. My only chore in the program was oversight and to accept the dividends of their efforts—and those men and women gave me an extraordinary team to lead.

Once you have their respect and your followers know they have yours, you'll begin to sense a change in energy. They will know that their success is your real goal. The next step in the process of closure will bring a long-awaited surge in momentum. You are right at the threshold of trust.

PART IV

PART *IV*

Trust

Nearly all men can stand adversity, but if you want to test a man's character, give him power.

–Abraham Lincoln

TRUST

Carrying a follower across the threshold of trust is magical. This is where the jets behind you begin to take the drag from your wake, where your people are close enough to remove weight from your efforts. Closing the gaps and crossing the trust barrier allows you to accelerate your team to a speed it could never have achieved another way. With proximity, however, comes risk. Even at highway speeds, followers who choose to move up inside a car length will be hard-pressed to shift their crosscheck away from the bumper in front of them.

Holding a position inside the trust barrier reduces situational awareness and reaction time to the point where there is no *safe separation*. If you collide with something here, there is little doubt that your follower will also be part of the wreckage. There were many moments in my career when I felt the surge of energy associated with the trust of an individual I was following, but few measure up to one specific night at the Pentagon.

I had worked for General Richard "Fig" Newton every day for the previous eight months when he called me into his office. The joint staff director of operations, General Douglas Lute, wanted to talk about air operations in Iraq, and Fig asked me to come along for the discussion.

General Lute started the meeting with a dire opening volley: things were looking grim in Iraq. He was aware of how thinly the Air Force was stretched and that we were barely able to sustain the training pipeline for replacement aircrews, but the situation in Iraq was about to become irreversible. We were losing ground, and if we didn't find a way to turn the tide, he felt we would lose the war. He asked if there was any way we could put more aircraft and personnel into the fight.

Increasing our numbers in the Persian Gulf was one of the most politically charged issues in the Pentagon, but General Lute was not playing politics. Like me he had just left the Gulf, and he knew the stakes better than anyone in the building. Anything Fig said in response would have repercussions. *Yes* would likely mean a backlash within our own service; but if he said *no,* I was convinced we would lose the fight. Before I finished that line of thinking, I was startled when Fig turned to me and said, "JV, what are your thoughts?"

The exchange was direct. I acknowledged and agreed with General Lute's assessment and went on to add my perspective. I had just left command of the Air Force Expeditionary Group that provided every strategic air-breathing reconnaissance aircraft and a large portion of the combat air power in the Gulf. In my opinion the reconnaissance assets we had in theater were not being used effectively, and I knew that the ground commanders would not give up those aircraft. Sending more aircraft into the Gulf to do the same thing might make the men and women on the ground *feel* more secure, but it would have no real effect on them or on the outcome of the war. The conversation that followed was remarkable.

As we stepped out of that room, the twinge of fear I had early on in the meeting was overwhelmed by the surge of energy that came from Fig. By willingly extending myself at his request, I had put myself at risk—and by handing me the reins of the conversation, he had put himself at risk within the organization. The surge came with mutual trust.

> **trust**
>
> The willingness to put yourself or your team at risk in the belief that another will follow through on a task, in a role, or with a mission.

Trust is the willingness to put yourself or your team at risk in the belief that another will follow through on a task, in a role, or with a mission. Expressions of trust that lack risk are merely expressions.

It had taken months to get there. We had developed commitment through countless discussions, tweaks in traction, and formal engagements. Over time Fig pulled me forward on my passions, his confidence, and a feeling of respect that brought me to the boundary—the threshold of trust. I had watched other people shift their positions (and allegiances) in similar roles, but every time I saw Fig under pressure he proved himself to be a man of integrity and stalwart principles. Would I have spoken up and put myself at risk without his trust?

There is a reason why it has taken seven chapters to reach the point where we are ready to break through the trust barrier. It takes time to override the biases—the internal layers of protection in others—and to give them reason to write new code that puts us on the precipice of trust. You have done a great deal of work on point, building commitment and earning your team's loyalty. You have coaxed them closer within your draft, and they have earned your loyalty. Now it comes down to your character.

Pulling key followers through the trust barrier relies on things that are already in place in your life. But your integrity and deep-seated principles will now be in full view of those closest to you in your draft. Prove worthy of their trust, and you will be amazed at the effects on your team— and at the surge of energy that comes as they move to take the drag from your wing.

CHAPTER 8

Close the Integrity Gap

ntegrity is how you add up, how your engagements with the pillars of faith, family, friends, health, and work measure up to the values you convey. Whether you set the markers for your values deliberately or unintentionally, they will become the metrics the team behind you will use to measure the leader they see.

Your interactions at work are the first thing your followers observe, but over time aspects of every pillar you value will be glimpsed. Every insight reveals more and more of who you are and unveils the mystery of your trustworthiness, one visible frame of reference at a time. Your followers will assume that what they see is congruent with your values—who you *really* are. The values your followers cannot see will be bolstered by, or fall victim to, what they *can* see.

> **integrity**
> How you add up. How your engagements with the pillars of faith, family, friends, health, and work measure up to the values you convey.

They will listen as you establish your expectations and values, and they will watch to see if you mate your actions with what you espouse. Match the two, and your integrity will lead them to cross the threshold of trust. The first time I consciously matched an individual's values with his actions in the Air Force came during my first months of flight school.

The first weeks at Sheppard Air Force Base in Texas were so compressed that it was easy to miss some of the details of that experience. Near the end of the third week, my attention rose up out of the pressure long enough to notice a bag of crushed aluminum cans in our flight room, and then I promptly fell back to the task at hand.

Several months later I was in the flight room well after everyone else should have been gone for the day. Startled by the sound of someone flattening a soda can, I looked over to see Major Paul Gruber putting it into a plastic bag. I had flown with him several times and felt comfortable enough to walk over and ask if he was doing something for his kids. He looked down for a moment, his face opened into a half smile, and said, "You might say that." I hope I never forget the story that followed.

Years earlier he had left the Air Force to join Braniff Airways. As fate would have it, it wasn't very long before airline deregulation and a faltering economy cost him that job. Several months without work drained his savings, and he had to find a way to feed his young family. Out of desperation he started going through dumpsters for aluminum cans to exchange them for cash at a recycling center.

When the Air Force finally accepted his application to rejoin the service, he made a promise to himself to never forget that period of his life and to never again take for granted the job of flying. He collected the cans to remind himself of what was really important. Major Gruber didn't pair his actions with his pillar of family for me—he did it for himself; but watching them match up helped me come to terms with the meaning of *integrity*. He was not just authentic and objective. The sum of his parts added up to someone I could trust.

Setting Expectations with the Thunderbirds

The prospect of learning to lead a 36-maneuver jet demonstration was incredibly intimidating. We started out with two jets flying side by side, 3 feet apart, executing one maneuver at a time. Half of my first sortie was spent flying a loop over and over again. As the demonstration leader, I wasn't working just on the pull or roll of the stick. Things happened fast when flying that close together, and sustaining our formation required every tip, every cue I could give the pilots on my wing. I had to learn how to tell my team what I was about to do and then execute that intent in a way they could follow.

The simplest things you can imagine had to be transmitted before I moved a muscle, and everything was said with a cadence.

"Smoke on ready—now."

"Smoke off ready—now."

"Release brakes ready—now."

"Burners—now."

All that was said just to start the takeoff roll. Once we were airborne, every movement of the stick or throttle was

preceded by a key of the mic: "Left turn . . . little more roll
. . . easing forward . . . power back . . ."

From brake release until we landed, I was on the radio
almost constantly.

As we began the thought process of closing the formations to airshow distances, the pilots on my wing were eval-
uating my every transmission and every turn. They listened
to the pace and tone of my delivery. They watched how my
actions mirrored my words, and, as you might imagine, they
were banking on the two adding up. My words formed *their*
expectations, and how my actions mirrored those words
determined whether the team would close in tight or keep
me at arm's length. The nuances were critical.

Your job likely doesn't require that you announce
your every move in advance, but what you do say will be
remembered. Whether it's your stated intent or the values
you silently convey, your team will be watching your every
move—and they will *not* be watching out of mere curiosity.

Your followers will take whatever insights you do
offer to form their own ideas of what you value and what
you don't. If you choose to not be direct, they will pick
up whatever inadvertent clues you drop to assemble their
picture of what you stand for. This is one of those figurative
black holes that will fill itself in if you let it. So long as you
are aware of that and, like Major Gruber, move with deliberate integrity, you're golden. But not everyone is that well
put together.

The Illusion of the Perfect Marriage

We were a startup division in a well-established consulting company, with the goal of breaking into new territory.

Hiring 17 people on the promise of new work was a big risk, but the company's president believed in our team leader, Billy "Big" Baggins. The pressure was on from day one, and during the first several months we burned a lot of midnight oil, trying to land our first contract. I was fortunate enough to capture the first win for our team, which seemed to make me one of Big's favorites.

He started dropping by my office to talk well after the rest of the staff had left for the day. The first several conversations were about the details of the contract and how hard he was working his network to find the next big lead. Over time our engagements began to change. He asked about my family and then bragged about his 30-year marriage. He asked about my involvement at church and then told me he had been a deacon in his own.

Then one night Big looked different, a little pensive. He walked in and, after pausing for a moment, said he needed to talk to someone, and then he unloaded. He and his wife had been living apart for several months. No one else in the organization knew it, but he didn't have many close friends and felt the need to share it with me. After a few consoling words, he expanded the *months* of separation into several *years*. He found himself spending a lot of time with an attractive woman at his country club—and he wanted to get my opinion on what he should do.

When he walked out that evening, I thought long and hard about his words. The way he had described his marriage in past conversations was the same way he talked about the other pillars of his life—the nuances and inflections were the same. While I couldn't be sure he devalued his other pillars in the same way, I knew my previous points of reference were, at best, less reliable.

Big may have needed a friend and a little sympathy that evening, but his revelations dismantled my overall faith in his word. The hair was standing up on my neck when I drove home that night.

Walking the talk   Consciously or unconsciously, we all look for tips or clues as to the strength of another's values. It is a survival instinct etched in our DNA. End a tense call with a family member, and the folks around you will be waiting for your next move: Point at the phone and say, "He'll make it work—I love that boy," and they'll get a feeling for how you value family. End it and say, "Idiot!" and, at the very least, they will use the moment as a proxy test* for what *they* can expect when they are on the other end of the line. If your move or response contradicts one of your stated values, that proxy test will expand to the pillars of your life that they can't see. Only the naive will assume the pillar they are in is exempt.

Being Intentional with Your Values

Being deliberate does not always mean *telling* people what you value, but it does mean being intentional about the pillars you allow those around you to see. Whether you reveal them directly or indirectly, the values you convey will set benchmarks for your team. How your actions

---

*Jeremy E. Sherman, PhD, wrote about the proxy test in a May 20, 2009, blog post for *Psychology Today* titled "Can I Trust Them? Here's the Quickest True Test."

match your values defines your integrity in the eyes of those behind you. Trust relies on your walking the talk.

Stating what you value is important, and there were at least 19 reasons to do that when I took the helm of the Thunderbirds. Before taking command, I read through the details of every major mishap in the Thunderbirds' history. In the 46 years prior to my command, 38 aircraft were lost, and 19 men died flying or learning to fly the demonstration. Some accidents were caused by mechanical failures, some by errors in judgment, and others by distractions away from the flight line.

In more recent years, the Thunderbirds suffered several near-misses that could have permanently tarnished the public image our mission was meant to build. Although the external damage receded from memory over time, the repercussions within the team lingered. Several prominent Thunderbirds had been fired, and two congressional investigations surrounding the team's professional conduct were ongoing. Senior Air Force leaders had removed from the demonstration maneuver package the team's signature diamond takeoff as well as several other formations. All of that had been lost because some individuals on previous teams had chosen to live outside the lines.

If the Thunderbirds continued down that same path, we would put something even bigger at risk—our trust in one another. We couldn't execute our mission without trust, and our job was to reinforce it with each other and to reclaim it with our leadership. From personal conduct off the field to every governing directive we were given, our team was going to live *inside* the lines. When we did that, we would claim the second goal for the years ahead: *to capture the confidence of kings*—both the confidence above us and the confidence within ourselves. It was my first objective as a leader: to make the Thunderbirds the most trusted organization in the Air Force.

Mindfully Conveying Your Values

More often than not, elevated goals and expectations yield opportunities for growth for the leaders on your team. The biggest of those opportunities involve you. Those in formation behind you have to carry the load of your stated values and take risks of their own to support them. If they get the sense that you are cavalier with your words, you will never get them to carry your water much less close the gaps that lead to trust.

Knowing that you can bank on your boss's word is a critical element of trust. Any fissures in his or her integrity will affect a lot more than your boss's trustworthiness. If you are close enough, your own integrity and that of *your* draft may end up taking significant collateral damage, as well. I learned that the hard way, with a rising star named Ken "Buck" Levins.

Backsliding from trust to loyalty   Buck was everything we could have hoped for. He was an excellent pilot, and that, coupled with his drive, temperament, and engaging personality, made him a perfect candidate for Fighter Weapons School (Top Gun). When I broached the topic with Buck, he could not have been more excited.

A short time later, Buck's name came out on another list—the one for Safety School. There was nothing he had done wrong; it was just timing—the slot opened and he was selected to fill it. Safety School all but ended a pilot's chances of making it to Fighter Weapons School, and we needed to get him off that list. I engaged my boss, Lieutenant Colonel Casey "Hawg" Jowles, to let him know the potential I saw in Buck, and I asked him to get someone else to fill the safety slot. He told me he would give it some thought.

Several weeks later we were flying night sorties, and I was one of the last two pilots to land. Hawg picked me up and then pulled the truck over while we waited for the last jet to pull into the chalks. It was a low-threat opportunity to check up on Buck's Safety School status; when I asked, Hawg confessed that he hadn't yet made a decision.

This one was important to me, and I told him that if he could let me win just one victory for my folks that year, I wanted it to be this one. I asked him, again, to pull Buck off the safety course so we could set him up for a future slot to Fighter Weapons School. He gazed out the windshield and commented on the evening—how the beautiful blue taxi lights were reflecting off the snow and what a memorable Christmas Eve this would be for both of us. "You'll get this one: I'll get him off the list."

Three months later Buck and I were airborne when a call went out on an emergency frequency for him to return to base immediately. By the time I touched down, he was already on his way to Seoul for a flight back to the States. I voiced my fears for his family but was quickly told that that was not the issue. His class start date for Safety School back in the States was the next morning—and somehow he hadn't gotten the word.

Hawg tried to tell me something must have slipped through the cracks at our headquarters, but, while that may have been true, I didn't believe him. He was someone I could no longer trust. It would be 10 weeks before Buck returned to our squadron, and I knew that no matter what I did or said, he would never trust me again. The Bank of Trust is a tough creditor: write a bad check and your good standing is gone forever.

Saying this, we are all human, and *you* might fail to live up to your word someday. What happens next? A failure in trust will cause those around you to back away. The additional space will give them more time to crosscheck the available positional cues and enough separation to maneuver around your *next* failure.

The very best we can hope to recover after a failure of our own integrity is loyalty. A follower's slide back from trust to loyalty will be so incremental that you won't feel the onset of drag, but your deceleration is inevitable. Come up short of your stated values or expectations a second time, and your followers will slide back from loyalty to commitment—or even disengagement. And they will stay there only until they can find another draft worth following.

Staying the Course

Integrity relies on your following the course you set for yourself, on your living up to and leading according to your own standards. Hold fast to your values, and you will not only sharpen your edge but also pull those trusting souls behind you even closer within your draft.

Things that can tempt you away from your integrity are everywhere. A pending promotion offers the opportunity for a small adjustment in your team's production numbers that might put you above the other candidates. Your boss asks you about a production line shutdown you could have prevented, and you subtly shift the blame to another department or to someone on your own team. The choices that reflect on integrity are plentiful, and most of them involve *pride*.

> ### pride
> Feelings of deep pleasure or satisfaction that arise from your achievements or from those of someone or something close to you.

One of my greatest temptations came just that way—a temptation of pride—in front of 100,000 people during the first airshow of my very first season.

Resisting the Temptation of Pride

The last three weeks of training season went well, and after three and a half months, the Thunderbirds got the green light to go on the road and commence the airshow season. The team's first show was in Tampa, Florida, and a massive crowd was there, enjoying what would be one of the best airshow days of the year. The weather was gorgeous, and flying at sea level meant our jet engines would perform at their very best. Aesthetics aside, the thrust available would make hitting the entry speeds for loops and rolling maneuvers much easier than in the thin air of the high desert. That thought was in the back of my mind as I rolled the four jets of the diamond formation to wings level and saw

that we were below the minimum entry airspeed for our
next maneuver.

"Power up . . . power *uuup.*"

As we flew over the point where I was supposed to
start the diamond loop, we were at 420 knots, 5 knots short
of the maneuver minimum. Big crowd, clear weather, lots of
thrust—I knew I could make it work—and then I realized I
couldn't. "The diamond will be straight through—airspeed."
I aborted the maneuver.

The crowd never knew the mistake was mine, but it
belonged to me alone. As we walked through the debrief
that evening, I popped in my cockpit camera footage and
talked as the frames detailed my error. There was little
doubt that with all the thrust available to us that day,
there was no reason for reaching my pull point below our
minimum speed. It was equally evident to everyone in the
room that I *could have* started the loop below the minimum
airspeed and we would have been just fine. A decision
just like that had led to a very public mishap in years past,
however, and it was important that the guys on my wing
knew I wouldn't cross the line and compromise our safety
standards—but it was even more important that *I* knew.

It was a humbling experience, but the incident and my
subsequent choices did something I could not have accomplished in any other way. It paired my actions and values
together in an honest moment—a moment I never could
or would have contrived. It showed my team that I could
be trusted. You cannot force evidence of your integrity on
those around you, and you don't get to choose the glimpses

others will use to substantiate their trust in you. You just have to live it.

As with the base of a lighthouse, the closer your team gets to your beam of light, the more of you they will see. Once you prove that your integrity is seamless, your followers will close to the point where they can see your deeply held principles. When they realize that your integrity is unshakable, they will be drawn in even tighter in your draft.

Close the Principle Gap

Having been convinced of your integrity, the folks in your draft are now close enough to catch glimpses of the deepest principles by which you live and operate and that inform your expectations. Their willingness to fully support the goals and directions they get from you will be based on what they see *in* you. They will watch how you lead, but they will also be close enough to see how you follow. They will study your fortitude as you move on the team's goals *and* on those of the parent organization, and they will fill in the unknowns—the gaps in principles they are able to see.

principle
A moral rule or belief that helps you know right from wrong and that dictates or helps shape your decisions and actions.

Principles are moral rules and beliefs that help you know right from wrong and that dictate or help shape your decisions and actions. To ensure that your principles continue to strengthen trust and entice closure, you must lead using *defined* principles—and build the kind of team that will challenge perceived shifts, slights, or failures in the principles your followers see in you.

Defending a Principle versus a Preference

Whether they are well defined or deeply buried in the recesses of our minds, principles guide us all. We received some through the basic coding of our lives, and we learned others through extraordinary example—both good and bad. Unfortunately, the most enduring principles form through failure, and most of us will wait to experience it before we cobble together an actual list of our moral rules and framing beliefs.

Tough Choices

The CEO's direction was clear, and his new president, Will Upright, had to make a very tough decision. Before Upright took action, he sought the advice of the leaders on his staff. He asked his senior vice presidents to provide papers summarizing the major points and impact as well as a bottom-line recommendation for their respective lanes. The VPs had seven days to get him their thoughts, and the president's decision meeting would take place a week later.

None of the choices was good, but one of them was particularly unsavory for *our* team. It would cut the operational budget to the point where we would have to shut down several critical efforts. Emotions intensified with every bullet our white paper took, but the recommendation was well supported and was exactly what our boss,

Vice President James "Lock" Turnkey, was looking for. He forwarded it on to the president.

A week later I escorted Lock down to the decision meeting and waited outside. He exited the room red faced and stormed back toward his office. Just as abruptly, he stopped in the middle of the hall, glared at me, and said, "If he thinks we're going to support that decision, he's out of his [*expletive*] mind!"

I was really attached to our recommendation but was taken aback by our vice president's words. We had been given the opportunity to state our case—we just didn't carry the day. The president's decision was grounded and well within his authority and the company's principles. Was Lock's outburst spurred by a principle, or a personal ***preference***—something he wanted more than another thing?

> **preference**
>
> A subjective feeling of liking or wanting something more than another thing.

Cascading Effects

We all have the right to pick and choose what we will and will not support, but the people behind us process everything they see. If you choose to disregard or even defy your boss, by proxy what options do you give the people behind you? Some will cling to your wing and hope you don't hit the bridge you're flying under, others will back away to get safe separation, but still others will move on their own preferences, the same way you did with yours.

Lock slowly eased away from President Upright and, over the next several months, undermined Upright's every move in the new direction. As I watched my boss slide back in the draft of *his* boss, my natural inclination was to match the distance. Even if you do not know the reasoning behind your boss's move, your senses will be screaming at you to back away in kind because you know something is not right. When you move to gain separation from your boss, so too will the folks in *your* draft.

By choosing to follow his own preference instead of the organization's principles, Lock injected a variant of organizational cancer that would weaken the entire organization.

Resisting the Temptation of Preferences

With your following at risk, what guides your decisions? And how do you lead those behind you through their own quandaries of conscience? Putting the success of an organization or the cohesion of a team at risk over a preference is a recipe for failure. Almost without thinking, however, people can elevate their preferences to the point where they carry the same weight as their principles. With well-seated preferences for every facet of our working lives, we can find ourselves at odds with virtually any decision.

What foundational standards do *you* use to guide your moves? What rules or codes of conduct dictate who you will—or what you won't—support? The only way to avoid an emotionally heated quandary is to take an inventory of your principles when you're not under pressure.

Taking an inventory of your principles If you were asked to write out the principles you lead by right now, you might be hard-pressed to come up with anything definitive. The Golden Rule or the Ten Commandments are common responses and, while the latter are exceptional principles, most of us would find it hard to name four. Principles are tough.

Preferences, on the other hand, are plentiful and easily named. From the type of movies we enjoy to the make and model of our cars, we have preferences for just about every facet of life. All things being equal, it is natural to want to hold on to the predictability of your own desires. The trap lies in becoming so attached to your preferences that you hold them as though they were principles.

Distinguishing among the Three Types of Principles

Personal principles, leadership principles, and organizational principles develop incrementally and are cumulative in both weight and effect. The strength of your personal principles bolsters your leadership principles, and the depth of the two together lays the foundation for organizational principles. Let's look at all three.

Personal Principles

Most things people consider principles are personal. "I will not lie, cheat, or steal" is a solid three-pack and, while you may have flirted with each during your early years, the worth of any follow-on principle you develop will

> **personal principles**
> Fundamental values that drive an individual's behavior and reasoning.

depend on your holding fast to those keyed in through your basic coding.

Personal principles are, well, personal. Even among siblings no two people have exactly the same ones. Whether you are looking at a boss or a subordinate, it is hard to tell if another has the same commitment you have to any personal principle. Right is right, and wrong is wrong, but moments and big events always give context to hard lines. With that it is important to take time to think before we react, or overreact, to what seems like an encroachment on a personal principle.

Several years ago I watched one of my bosses move on a principle that, I believe, was taken at face value—and the lack of context cost our little team a great deal.

Hiring 17 people on the promise of new work was a risk for our consulting company, but the company's president moved to take it. He assured our team leader, Big Baggins, that he would have the latitude to hire as many people as he needed, and the only caveat he gave Big was to turn a profit within two years. Our first contract was rapidly expanding, and it was set to cover the full-time salaries for nine team members and the part-time salaries for another four. We weren't making a profit yet, but we were getting closer by the day.

Late one afternoon Big stormed into my office. He looked ashen and blurted out the words, "He lied!" The president was no longer going to give us two years to make a profit. We now had 18 months, and that deadline was just four months away.

I acknowledged Big's frustration and asked him how close he thought we were to actually making a profit.

"That's beside the point. He lied, JV! He *lied!*"

"Big, I think we're awfully close to giving him what he wants. Is there any way the president could be upping the ante because of the confidence he has in you and our team?"

"You don't get it—he lied!"

One of Big's personal principles had been violated, and he was beside himself. The next day he called our 17-member team into a meeting. With that same defeated expression, he told us if we weren't already working on a project full-time, we needed to find another job. As you might imagine, that all but destroyed our draft.

What our team didn't know—and what our boss seemed not to have considered—was the *context* for the president's change in direction. There were a dozen things that could have been driving the shift in deadlines. Looming cash shortfalls driven by a collapsing customer in another division could have caused him to pull back some of our allotted time. Or the president could have been considering Big for a promotion to an executive VP role—or even his own—but he wanted to see him under pressure before he made the move. Context is important, and the integrity of your boss's draft—and yours—means giving your leader your complete support through the point where you know the context of his or her decision.

Defining your personal principles   It is up to you to determine what constitutes a personal principle, but stay true to yourself and narrow yours down to the traits you *really* value. For principles to mean something to you, they need a lineage or pedigree. Personal principles generally come from the upbringing you received from parents or other caregivers, and that lineage offers a powerful start. With that as a foundation, you can build and hold fast to the principles beyond.

Leadership Principles

Unfortunately, many people will not take the time to articulate their own **leadership principles** until they come face-to-face with a significant emotional event. Every nerve-shaking incident or failure presents the opportunity to add or refine leadership principles that you use to guide your actions. I had had my fair share of principle-shaping events by the time I joined

> **leadership principles**
> Basic rules and beliefs that guide a leader's actions.

the Thunderbirds, and, as fate would have it, within my first year on point the resolve of one of them was being tested on several fronts.

Lieutenant Colonel Frank "Ball" Park had crossed the line a third time. This time he had flown 15 feet over the heads of a group of people while he was in full afterburner.*

His first strike had been a low pass level with the T-tail of a four-engine C-5 Galaxy, 65 feet over the top of our folks on the ground. The second strike came when he flew his own version of a knife-edge pass beneath the wide eyes of tower controllers perched 80 feet off the ground.

With a photo of his third strike in hand, I now knew he could not respect the principles I set for the Thunderbirds. That was issue enough, but he was also living so far

---

*An *afterburner* is an additional chamber mounted behind jet engines, where fuel is injected and ignited to deliver a surge in thrust.

outside our governing directives and flying regulations that he would have lost his wings in any other squadron.

The perils of failing to act   I had seen something like this before—a series of unchecked actions that eventually manifested in an accident in North Carolina. Like every other mishap, that one had a story line, a series of events that built on one another. I watched several leaders avoid taking action in the hope that the situation would resolve itself or because of the turmoil it might cause in their careers. Any act beyond the bounds of principle that is not reset allows the next (potentially bigger one) to come to life. Without breaking the chain, these leaders allowed fate to dictate the outcome, and that cost the lives of 26 people. If any one of them had had courage enough to break the chain, we could have avoided that horrible ending. I left that wing a year later with my first real leadership principle: *Never let your failure to act put another at risk.*

Leadership principles are important, but their job, and yours, is to further the goals and principles of the organization.

Organizational Principles

Organizational principles are the foundational beliefs that fuel a company's mission, values, goals, and its day-to-day behavior. Having your own team principles, or list of values that frame your expectations, may seem a little over the top for a small group, but

> **organizational principles**
> The foundational beliefs that fuel a company's mission, values, and goals and its day-to-day behavior.

putting them in the form of goals is something that most will embrace. When it comes right down to it, organizational principles and goals serve the same purpose, and if your goals are not your principles, they should embody every one of them. Every personal and leadership principle you craft lays the foundation for the next higher tier, and every organizational principle you spell out should point back to and serve the needs of your goals.

I had briefed my boss following Ball's previous flying violations along with my plan to bring him in line. When I showed him the picture of Ball's third strike, he shook his head. "He's an idiot," he said. "I can't believe he would be so foolish." And then just as quickly he looked up and asked, "Can you keep him?"

Choosing the easy road or the rough one   There is not a leader out there who wouldn't choose to minimize the production breakdowns, industrial accidents, and personnel problems that we are paid to prevent. But if you move to fix a problem before it manifests into something everyone can see, you will create the kind of turmoil most organizations don't enjoy or promote.

When you stand by your principles, you will often feel like you are standing by yourself—and there is a good chance you are doing just that. If the issue is large enough, your boss may feel threatened by your stance, but his or her angst is only one aspect of the pressure you'll face. There is a strong possibility that those behind you will see your stance either as uncalled for or as change they don't want—and that weight can be significant.

The politics surrounding any hard call can run deep, and even in situations where someone is breaking the law, your decision to take action can be as costly for you as it is for the one who steps outside the lines. It takes courage to follow through on hard calls, and there are examples every day in the news that highlight the need for integrity of principles: leaders who draw red lines and then quietly let them fade back into the terrain, politicians who change the context of their promises, and parents who overlook their child's increasingly dangerous behavior. The strength of your draft in any realm relies on your holding fast to your principles.

"Can you keep him?"

Really? "No, sir, I can't."

The way the Thunderbirds were manned, if we kept him on, Ball would either rise up to become the keeper of the rules, or he would keep his current job and continue to fly unsupervised. Neither option was viable.

"Right—that wouldn't make sense." Then my boss asked me again, *"Can you keep him?"*

Challenges to your principles will come from all sides, and your principles need to be seamless to meet them. That requires thought on your part regarding the values you carry and how they affect the team itself.

There was a time in my career when I, like Ball Park, lived on the other side of directives, but we were not lieutenants anymore, and our mission was to set the standard for the Air Force. The only way to meet our goal of capturing the confidence of kings was to live it every day, and I could no longer trust Ball to do that on his own. He had been given clear direction and two chances—two strikes—to realign his preferences with the principles I had laid out, but he would not do it.

Applying Your Principles

Once your principles are in place, you need a method for using them to make the hard calls. In the purest sense, if an issue doesn't compromise a principle, it must be a preference. While that sounds good on paper, the gray areas of the real world rarely allow for black-and-white answers. There will always be issues you recognize as preferences and others that cross well into the world of principles. Assuming that you recognize your clear preferences and have the wherewithal to act on principle, the challenge lies in the gray areas in between. Unfortunately, more issues than you might think lie in that middle ground (see Tough Decisions).

Tough Decisions: *The Grays between Principle and Preference*

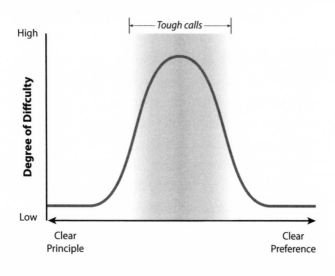

Some preferences are so well ingrained that they don't *feel* like preferences. Equally troubling is the fact that some encroachments on your principles will be of such a low grade that it may not seem like they are under assault at all. We therefore need a plan for sorting the wheat from the chaff.

Asking Yourself: Is This a Principle?

Just by asking yourself the question *Is this a principle?*, you will bring rational thought to situations in which emotions can take control. Your final answer must be clear, but take your time getting there because the thresholds between principles are key.

Personal principles are important, but few people are raised with the same basic coding as others, so it's likely your personal principles will be different from those of your followers. That said, your coding is you, so use those lines to establish your own bounds of trust.

Leadership principles are critical, but they also serve a greater master. The leadership principles you establish support the organizational principles your team needs you to see through. If someone is violating a leadership principle, *name* the principle he or she is violating. If he or she cannot be trusted to lead your people to the goals you establish, it would be foolish to give, or keep, that person in a significant position of leadership on your team.

The organization's principles—its mission, values, and goals—are what every team member signed on to serve. If someone is disengaged or living so far outside the lines that his or her actions put the organization at risk, that person needs to go.

If you cannot name the principle an individual has violated, it may be your own well-seated preference that is at issue. That doesn't mean it's unnecessary to adjust your follower's trajectory a bit, but it downgrades considerably the severity of the situation.

Seeing Principles at Work

Lieutenant Colonel Ball Park had crossed my personal and leadership principles, and he had walked all over the team's goal of capturing the confidence of kings. There was no question: this *was* a matter of principle.

What were the repercussions of inaction? If Ball clipped the tail of another aircraft during a low pass, he might survive the ejection, but there was no predicting the collateral damage he would cause. Even if the physical losses were limited to a $20 million jet, the damage to the professional image of the Air Force would be severe.

My boss's question was hanging in the air. Could I *not* take action on a man clearly living that far outside the lines? The easy answer was no, absolutely not. But if that were true, how could I have given him a pass after his first strike much less the second? If I could give Ball two strikes, what's so critical about the third?

I had confronted Ball's second strike well armed. A senior Thunderbird had witnessed the low pass and had come forward to let me know about the incident. I called the tower at the airfield where it happened, and the details the tower controller provided were a perfect match to the first account: a knife-edge pass, flown just below the big glass windows of the control tower.

When I had confronted Ball over that second incident, he gave me a line so simplistic that it was condescending: "Sir, I'm new to the F-16, and I would never feel comfortable flying *that* low *that* fast in this aircraft."

Something I had said in the discussion that followed changed his disposition; he dropped the facade and admitted that he had flown the low pass just as I had described.

Now with a third strike, I could offer a measure of compromise, predicated on one more assessment of character. I told my boss I would engage Ball in my office. Ball knew I had the photograph of his third strike, so if he came clean, showed remorse, and then asked for one more chance, I would consider giving him a fourth strike. If he didn't, I would relieve him on the spot.

When I handed Ball the photo of his third strike, I asked if it was a picture of him. He looked concerned for a moment and then, unbelievably, he repeated the same line he had used with his second strike: "Sir, I'm new to the F-16, and I would never feel comfortable flying *that* low *that* fast in this aircraft."

I relieved him right then and there.

The weight and repercussions surrounding that decision were significant, but living by and leaning on principle gave me peace of mind.

The integrity of *your* personal, leadership, and organizational principles will deliver something more than a logical decision train. They will help organize and ground your thoughts, and the decisions that result from that process will have a level of certainty and weight of confidence you'll get no other way. Once your process is in place, all you need is a game plan for putting that footing to work.

Leading with Principles

Some system failures in the F-16 were annoying, but others would get your full attention. Just getting a crippled jet close to our home field outside Madrid, Spain, was comforting on several fronts, but perhaps the biggest reassurance came with the *voice* that emanated from the control tower. He was more like a guardian angel than the chief controller, and he always seemed to be there for us as things turned south. For whatever reason, when Senior Master Sergeant Michael "Iron Mike" Carbonneau came up on the radio, you knew everything was going to be okay. We had worked together countless times, but there was one particular day when Iron Mike proved he was driven by the highest ethics and principles at work—principles that helped prevent a bad day from becoming tragic.

The weather was unusually bad for Madrid, which didn't bode well for my looming shift as the supervisor of flying. When I showed up in the tower, the guy I was replacing didn't seem very concerned. "Sixteen jets are airborne, and the field is VFR."

VFR, or *visual flight rules,* was supposed to mean our ceiling was 3,000 feet and the visibility better than 3 miles. I wasn't a weatherman, but I could not see either end of the runway, and if we had 3,000 feet, they were newborn-baby feet. The problem was that nobody airborne had known to carry extra fuel for what was ahead. I was in trouble.

As if on cue, Iron Mike appeared out of nowhere: "Just off the phone with our weather shop. Visibility is just under 2 miles, the observed ceiling is 400 feet, and everything's dropping. I've got the forecast for the last viable alternate airfield, and it is not good. What can I do to help?"

Working together we recovered 10 jets at home and got the other six into that alternate field 140 miles away. The weather at both fields was bad when the jets arrived, and each pilot flew an approach down to, or below, his weather minimum—and the best of the lot landed at the alternate with less than six minutes of fuel remaining. While they were all thankful to make it back on the deck, I was really the only pilot who knew how bad it had been—and or whom to thank.

Iron Mike didn't work for me, and we weren't even in the same chain of command. He could have rightfully focused his efforts on supervising *his* staff and working the challenges within *their* pattern, but he trusted his shift supervisor to watch over our field. He was there, just as he always was, to make sure the goals of *our* wing were fulfilled again that day. It was not an organizational chart that was driving that man, it was the principle by which he led his team—to support the mission of our wing in every way they could.

Leading by Example

Writing down and sharing your team's goals and values is an important move in the engagement process, but the biggest is through your example. The 16 pilots who were airborne that afternoon in Spain may have been the biggest beneficiaries of Carbonneau's efforts, but the most important audience was his team of controllers. He showed them, once again, that their team goals were subordinate to our wing's goals. He could have taken a much easier, more selfish path. Lock Turnkey, the vice president who undermined his boss's goals for the sake of his own, took that path, and the effects on *his* draft were crippling. Iron Mike's draft was incredible.

Live your principles and build your own plan for applying them.

Mistakes and Other Matters

Even your most diligent followers will make mistakes. The severity of those missteps will vary like the extremes of principles and preferences. Some errors will be so small that they are worth nothing more than a raised eyebrow; others will be so severe that your hands will be tied, but those that fall in the middle require a game plan. Your patience, and that of your organization, may allow multiple failures of one type or another, but remember that the rest of your team is watching. If you lower your standards, your draft will suffer, so there must be a balance.

No matter how early or late you make a call or take corrective action, there will always be people who second-guess you. The idea is to design something that works—that you can remember, repeat, justify, and live with. Design your plan to realign errant behavior any way you like, but be sure to incorporate the big picture into your crosscheck. Mistakes, like failures, offer unrivaled opportunities for growth. Build in steps that allow a person who slipped up to grow from the experience and get back in the race. Of course, if there are repetitive failures, you need a method for delivering increased levels of training and guidance until your people get it right. For the more serious issues, the three-strikes scheme similar to the one I used with Ball Park works well. It relies on your communicating your expectations up front and then scaling your response in a way that is clear to everyone.

It is not likely that many people in your draft have developed their own list of principles much less a method for applying them. Unless you coach them on yours and give them a clear picture of your expectations, you may keep them off balance. Apprising the folks behind you of both your principles and your method enables them to close with confidence. And once they know that your principles are unshakable, they will continue forward with the intent of removing every fleeting ounce of drag from your efforts.

The insights and perspectives that your most trusted followers can offer at this point of closure are more valuable than ever, but the conditions must be right for them to speak up.

Building Friction into Your Following

It is in our DNA as leaders to take well-intended questions as challenges to our authority, particularly in high-pressure situations. Giving your people the freedom to voice their opinions and concerns without the fear of being pummeled relies on your developing a healthy level of *friction* within your team.

> **friction**
>
> Refining or challenging a thought, proposed course of action, or direction through a suggestion, statement, or question.

While I was learning the Thunderbird demonstration during training season, I knew that, with all the moving parts, there was a good chance I could get wrapped up in my own thoughts and miss something critical. One of the first indicators that that was happening came over the radio. Hundreds of transmissions were required during a 30-minute demonstration, and if I missed or botched two radio calls in close order, there was a good chance I was behind the power curve. If I missed three, there was no doubt.

Slam Byrne, my operations officer, picked up on that cue in the first few weeks of training. He developed the habit of questioning my status after the second error, and, whenever he asked, there was no doubt in my mind that he was right.

Over time that three-strike playbook became part of the demonstration, and anyone could make the challenge. No matter where we were in the routine or how enamored I was with some aspect of our maneuvering, that wake-up call worked.

The noise surrounding operations can get pretty intense, and at times even the most ominous warnings can be lost or explained away amid the clamor of just making things happen. That roar can become deafening when you are under stress. In the movie *It's a Wonderful Life*, the druggist Mr. Gower was under stress when he accidentally put poison in capsules meant for a family. It took George Bailey two brutally rebuffed attempts before he got his boss to wake up and realize what he was doing.

During your own "Mr. Gower moments," who on your team has the fortitude and the trust it takes to sound that claxon for you? While you're stewing on that question, let me sneak in another story that may bring more life to this issue. It was a morning rife with every operational and supporting peacetime challenge I could imagine, and I didn't handle it well.

A bad morning   The weather had not allowed us to turn
a wheel all weekend, and the trip home was looking equally
dismal. Flying instruments in inclement weather can be
challenging, but taking off in bad weather with a formation
of single-seat fighters has a few added complications. Every
wingman must follow his instruments while simultaneously
using his radar to find the jet in front of him. Once he does
that, his job is to close to 2 miles in trail and stay there—and
every aspect of the process can be disorienting.

I had participated in dozens of radar trail departures
that had gone well and a few that had not. The more aircraft
and the more turns that are involved, the less likely a trail
departure can be executed effectively.

After 45 minutes of waiting for two instrument
clearances, only one came out of the system, and it was for
eight jets. I had already briefed my team that we would not
fly a departure with eight aircraft that morning. The plan
was to go with two flights of four jets, but for some reason
the thought of taking eight entered my mind. As we taxied
out, my operations officer keyed his radio and voiced his
concern: "What are we doing?"

I processed the question and his tone internally but
somehow twisted what he meant as a warning into the need
for detail on how we were going to execute an eight-ship
departure. Just like Mr. Gower, I missed my first cue, and
it came from a man I trusted more than any other. There
would not be a second.

Taking off with eight jets that morning was a mistake
that was mine alone. It was through no small amount of
luck that we all made it home safely that afternoon, but the

incident would stay with me for months to come. In thinking back on it with the clarity of hindsight, I realized the need to better arm those behind me.

Some details are so big you should never lose track of them, but in your quest to be right—when you absolutely *know* you are right—you can drop some of the most obvious from your crosscheck. In those moments giving someone you trust the means to intervene on your behalf can save much more than your pride.

Empowering people to step in and challenge your principled decisions can do more than save you a little embarrassment, but you have to control it. Give that power only to your most trusted followers and then build in a checks-and-balances system of your own.

Giving Your Most Trusted "All-Stop" Cards

Soccer fans know that when a referee pulls out a yellow card, he has spotted something out of sorts that is significant enough to temporarily suspend play. Issuing yellow cards (whether real or figurative) to leaders holding the knowledge, judgment, and wherewithal to use them can be a real accelerant. Empowering them with that kind of weight and giving their voices that kind of influence will bring them even closer. Still, you want to control it.

Load their accounts with just one yellow card at a time, and there can be no doubt in your mind when they use it: "This is a yellow-card event for me." If you take the time to set up your own Mr. Gower, or yellow-card, system you *must* respect the individual's move when he or she shows that level of concern. Reloads of the cards are predicated on their effective and responsible first use.

Once it is in place, a system like this will show the people behind you that you deeply value their judgment. You will not just close the principle gap but will have your organization poised at the edge of maximum performance.

Close the Empowerment Gap

You have done it! You have moved your team from the first steps of commitment to the deepest layers of trust. Once your key players cross beyond the threshold and break the trust barrier, you will feel the surge in energy all around you. Along the way you have instilled an incredible foundation—one that will allow you to close the last gap in your draft.

Your job now is to charge those closest to you with growth-filled opportunities that require your authority to execute. Pairing the right opportunity with the right skill sets and passions can deliver huge dividends. It will free you up for other tasks and allow you to plan and execute an elevated trajectory for your team. The collective effects will not only deliver mutual acceleration but also allow you to sustain a speed that you and your team could never have achieved before.

Those behind you will be caught up in the same surge of energy that you are feeling. For some the challenge of just staying there will be enough. Others will have so

much energy that you'll find yourself challenged to keep
up with their need for growth. And still others will top out
and choose to pursue other passions or paths. Powering
up every team member and helping them close on their
long-term needs and passions—even if those lay outside
the organization—will have an extraordinary impact on
the caliber of new hires that enter your draft. The first stage
of that effort is your last step in the move to 18 inches of
closure: empowerment.

Empowerment

Empowerment is granting your authority to a subordinate
for the execution of a significant task, based on and framed
by the expectations, resources,
boundaries, and guidance
you give.

empowerment
Granting your authority to a subordinate for the execution of a significant task, based on and framed by the expectations, resources, boundaries, and guidance you give.

Any level of empowerment
involves risk. Remember that golf
course with the terrible cheeseburgers? You could argue that the
risk Leo Van Wart took on when
he empowered his cooks to create
a better burger was low, but that
depends on your perspective. If
you are trying to start a fire, kindling is very important. If
it fails to catch or hold a flame, you can miss out on a bit of
atmosphere on an otherwise romantic evening—or you can
freeze to death. For an organization that was teetering on
insolvency, Leo needed the cooks in his grill to catch.

The risks you are willing to assume with empowerment can run the gamut, but anytime you take that step, launch the effort on the foundation of commitment, loyalty, and some degree of trust before you give your authority to another.

For the key leaders behind me on the Thunderbirds, empowerment meant assigning them tasks with specific expectations for delivery. Because of the lanes within and beyond our hangar walls, I gave them clear boundaries to operate in without my direct supervision. From there my job was to give them resources, guidance, and encouragement to see the task through. Freeing them from my day-to-day oversight in those roles took a significant amount of weight from our respective shoulders. An example or two here will help you frame your own empowering efforts.

Meeting Expectations

One of the key pillars of the goal to double the Thunderbirds' exposure to the public was to capture a cereal box featuring the team. While we probably would have settled for any cereal, I gave Guy Hunneyman the target of Kellogg's Frosted Flakes. Toddlers to teenagers enjoyed them, and if we reached that group, we'd be hitting our target audience with images of the team the first thing every morning.

Guy was leaving at the end of our first year together, so he and his team had nine of those months to bring that box home. Make sure you include a specific deadline with your expectations, as few open-ended timelines pay off.

Setting Boundaries

Salespeople are given territories, specific sectors of government, or a list of clients to develop. The bounds for empowerment in that field are no different in that your followers need to know the limits of their authority as well as how long they will have it.

One of the unusual things about the leadership of the Thunderbirds was that there were few occasions when I could see, much less focus on, all the jets on my wing. That meant when I was flying the demonstration, I could not be in charge of safety, nor could I direct ground movements or maintenance actions or interface with air-traffic control. When I was airborne, my operations officer was empowered to run the entire operation. He had the authority of a commander until I was back on the ground.

Marshaling Resources

The Thunderbirds didn't actually have a budget to expand our impact for the Make-A-Wish Foundation, nor did we have funds to incorporate data-link systems into our fleet of jets. Knowing that, and then watching the two men I empowered move on their respective challenges, was flat-out inspiring.

With a bit of luck, you will actually have funds, equipment, and teammates to further any effort that you empower. Make sure your followers know what they have and where the hard stops are.

Providing Guidance

While boundaries and resources both include some level of direction, make sure you bat cleanup here with recommendations for whom to engage for support, what your role is in their effort, and when they need to touch base with you. You can give your *authority* to others, but you cannot give up your responsibility, so build in regular checkpoints for your followers to brief you on their progress, problems, and proposed solutions. Once you have those in place, they need to know that you believe in them—and that you are confident that they can accomplish the task.

Believing in Your Team

Unexpected mires and barriers of all sorts will manifest to meet any worthy effort, and you need to make sure your people know you have faith that they will see it through. Individuals you empower will be plowing the path for the team behind them—and it's easy to get discouraged in that role. Give them your presence, support, and encouragement—but don't back away from your expectations. The growth those situations offer is incredible, and the dividends waiting for your team on the other side of those barriers can be huge.

Two months after it had approved our plan to use a background story of cancer to capture several TV news magazines, the Air Force backed away from the initiative. We could no longer use my battle with cancer and the name *Thunderbirds* in the same sentence. With that, the surge of excitement behind our 20-million-person goal began to fade. It was a page out of the Leo Van Wart playbook that brought the team back on task. I continued to hold on to the objective and to praise their efforts in everything from all-hands meetings to one-on-one engagements. *Faith* is the belief in something unseen—and I did my best to let Guy know that he could make it happen without the crutch of cancer.

Once the people you empower know that you believe in them, the effects of their efforts can be startling.

Leo's advertising campaign for "the best cheeseburger in town" successfully lured scores of people to his grill. The first several waves walked out frustrated, but their dissatisfaction and that of those who followed delivered the intended affect. Over time Leo's mantra of "the best cheeseburger in town" drove his cooks back to the grill. When they were finished, those two men had crafted five different gourmet burgers that really did bring in people in droves.

Once the grill came up to speed, Leo shifted his loving heat to the pro shop and then the greenkeepers. Over time every other profit center in the golf complex was touched by the expectations of the others. The fairways thickened, the greens began to roll like carpet, and the driving range turned into a plush oasis. And the cheeseburgers? *Our* cheeseburgers were the best in town.

What Trust and Empowerment Did for the Thunderbirds

There were more individual and organizational triumphs that came out of our two-year draft than I could rightly capture in this book, but four accomplishments stand out. Each was the product of extraordinary efforts and a team that defined the word *trust*.

A Wish for Make-A-Wish

Our left wingman, Chase Boutwell, was like a duck on the water—you could never see how hard he was paddling, but he was always driving hard and fast. Our first three weeks of Friday practice airshows had a solid turnout of Make-A-Wish families, but after that the numbers seemed to grow significantly. It was his direct outreach that made that happen, and it turned those mornings into the most gratifying events of the show season.

Chase was hired for just one year, but he proved himself to be as solid they come. He was an exceptional pilot in the air, and he showed his resilience and character every day on the ground. His efforts with Make-A-Wish earned the team the foundations' National Award for Public Service, which gave us more than a little positive national exposure. Convincing our leadership that Chase should stay for two more years as the slot pilot was one of the easiest, most enjoyable, and beneficial sells of my tenure.

Securing a Live Wire for the Internet

Our maintenance officer, Hawk Hawkins, was very resourceful and driven to make our video idea a success. He found that the Air Force supply system was flush with parts for a dated data-link system, and that young officer convinced the suppliers to give us the parts for free. After a little more due diligence, we had the nod to go forward.

Six months after Hawk took on the task of fleshing out the requirements, we began modifying the aircraft. Our new digital data-link system, which integrated live cockpit video with our ground crew's footage, was ready for the Internet.

The following season the video was being shown on Jumbo-trons at show sites across the United States.

Capturing the Confidence of Kings

During his year as my operations officer, Slam Byrne's constant oversight and direct prods were a godsend for the team as a whole but particularly for me as the commander. Through the thousands of maneuvers and repositions over the course of a full demonstration season, we had just one rub,* and that came on the most turbulent day of the season—otherwise the team flew clean throughout the year.

Slam was the one empowered to make first contact in the world of operations—and that took a huge weight off my shoulders. His actions helped put the team back inside the lines and ensured that we lived the standards we espoused. Halfway through that year, we added one of our lost maneuvers, the diamond formation takeoff, back into our demonstration portfolio. From that point on, the leadership had little reason to question our discipline in the air or on the ground. We won their confidence and, with it, we gained our own: the confidence of kings.

Increasing the Direct Exposure of the Team

Even after we lost our crutch of cancer, Guy Hunneyman flew to Battle Creek, Michigan, repeatedly to entice, engage, negotiate, and finally seal a deal that would capture a cereal box featuring the Thunderbirds. For the months following its release, kids from the age of three to 18 would wake up

---

*Rubs, or paint swaps, occur when jets actually make contact in the air, leaving paint where the rub occurred.

to a breakfast of Kellogg's Frosted Flakes cereal and images of our team. We were hoping Kellogg would print a million boxes, but the effort exceeded our wildest expectations: they printed 40 million.

Guy didn't just double the direct exposure of the Thunderbirds to the public. He and his team increased it by more than a factor of four, and the seeds he planted for the Air Force will be showing up at the doors of recruiting offices for years to come. Guy did all that in a job that he thought was mundane—one he was using as stepping stone to his lifelong dream. Can you imagine what he's doing now for the Federal Bureau of Investigation?

Sometimes Empowerment Means Helping Someone Leave

Once you have people accelerating in your draft, you must continually challenge them as they move forward. If you don't have a significant task to empower them toward or a position you can promote them into, expect their frustration. When that happens your options are to keep them where they are (hold them back), watch them seek out another job, or help them find their next position.

Your followers will feel any semblance of an effort on your part to hold them back, and when they do they'll realize that it is just *your* dreams that are important—something that will compromise your draft. Turning a blind eye as they surreptitiously seek their next job is an option, but why would you stop encouraging them forward at this point? The best of all options is to help them find their next landing spot.

Many parent organizations, like the US Air Force, have career programs and progression paths. If your company does, finding a position that will challenge the rising stars behind you may be relatively easy. The rub comes when there are no internal billets for them, or a follower is determined to leave the organization. When that happens don't give up the fight. I watched with amazement one of the best leaders I have ever known pull strings for a man who was bound and determined to leave the Air Force. That man was me.

The Real Power of Drafting

It was the eighth month of my assignment to Kunsan Air Base, and I was approaching a cliff. During my eight years in the Air Force, I had met a few extraordinary leaders but more than my share of those falling short of what I needed to stay. I took the assignment to Korea with the intent of its being my last post in the service, and the deadline for accepting or rejecting my next assignment was at hand. It would have been an easy decision eight months earlier— before I ran into Colonel John "Grumpy" Miller, the wing commander at Kunsan.

Grumpy was everything I enjoyed in a leader. He was an exceptional pilot in the air, and he made things happen on the ground. He didn't suffer fools, and when he saw something good or someone who was driven, he did everything he could to further their efforts. Even so, my experience told me he was an anomaly, and after seven days of continual butterflies, I elected to separate. That decision didn't go over well with our wing commander.

Grumpy was angry, disappointed, and relentless. It was our third meeting, and I was emotionally wrung out. The banter began the same way it had in our previous meetings, with him throwing my separation papers at me, asking, "What the [*expletive*] do you want me to do with these?!"

"I want you to sign them."

"So, after what you've seen this year, you don't think the Air Force has good leaders?"

"You're an anomaly."

He repeated his offer to help get me into Fighter Weapons School, to watch over me for the rest of my career, but then, seeming resigned to the outcome, his tone completely changed.

"I realize I probably can't keep you, but I want to keep your talents as close to the Air Force as I can. I want you to know that if you choose to leave the active duty Air Force, I've arranged for you to have a job with the Alabama Air National Guard, full- or part-time, if you want it. You'd be flying the same jets you're flying now in your home state. From there, JV, I'll help you any way I can."

He asked me to come back the next day with my decision, and, if I still wanted to leave the service, he would sign my paperwork.

When I left that afternoon, I was caught up in a wave of emotion so powerful that it was hard to hold back the tears. I had been in the service for eight years, and during that time no one I worked for had been willing to take this big of a risk or go this far out of his way to help me.

Grumpy used every bit of positive leverage he had to keep me from leaving his team. But even after I told him

I wanted out, his belief in me didn't end. He took it upon himself to give me the best landing outside the Air Force that I could have wished for, where I would continue to live one of my life's greatest passions by flying the F-16.

Grumpy really was an anomaly, and the pull of his draft, his empowering belief, was so strong that I could not leave. I walked in the next afternoon and told him I would stay.

As odd as it may seem, getting someone placed with an organization that may even be your competition can be an exceptional personnel move. For starters, if you go out of your way to place people you've trained, their level of trust will rise to a point where they realize they may not find another Grumpy Miller on any other team. That is one reason why I elected to stay in the Air Force for another 15 years.

Even if someone accepts your help and leaves your organization, having a trusted colleague on a respected competitor's team can be a huge advantage. Other stars will continue to grow rapidly in your draft, and they will need a place to go. Having a trusted teammate in the professional network beyond your team will make your next placement a bit easier. As things go, those who leave will respond in kind with insights and recommendations on high-quality folks from their new organization who would be great fits in yours.

And then there is the effect on those around your team. Once they hear that your following wind won't end with their tenure, that you really are out for their best interests, people will fight to join you. Your ability to hire even more qualified candidates will grow, as will your ability to continually increase your team's speed, the quality of the goods or services you produce, and the strength of the bond of those in your draft.

The power of drafting is real.

In looking back, people just like Grumpy Miller had been perfectly placed throughout my career. Every person and every pivotal event seemed to come at the ideal time. Some pulled me forward, and others put their following to work with their own closing efforts. The energy associated with each allowed me to witness the warmth, the increasing speed, and the incredible power of drafting.

Epilogue

My thoughts filled the cockpit as we taxied to the runway to begin the final act of the show at Andrews Air Force Base—and I was beaming. At the start of training season, the distance between jets was the same as we had flown throughout our operational lives, but then we had hardly known each other. Closure had come at a glacial speed as we waited for the lines of coding to settle in—the coding of commitment, then loyalty, and finally the kind of trust that would allow us to give up the peripheral cues and the safe separation on which our lives had depended. We gave them up every time we took off, out of trust in one another, and we were about to do it again.

I returned Mo Southern's salute and watched his crew clear the runway in a light drizzle. Looking up, I saw the sky was still a mess. The conservative call was to stay beneath the clouds and try to satiate the hunger of the crowd with a whole lot of jet noise—but holes in the weather were opening up, and there was a chance we could create a memory that would last a lifetime.

On my right Skid Greene was nodding rhythmically, and beyond him Chase Boutwell flashed his signature double-deuce. On my left wing, Doug "Animal" Larsen's thumbs-up framed a smile leaking out the sides of his mask. We were ready.

We broke ground and quickly climbed through a break in the first layer of clouds. As I started the reposition for the diamond formation's opening maneuver, I looked over my left shoulder, and, miraculously, the low cloud deck was gone.

"Setting up for the high show"—"two, three, four, five, six—*seven!*" We were on.

The pockets of billowing cumulus that remained formed a breathtaking landscape, but one that removed any chance we could fly the ground track we had practiced hundreds of times before. For 30 minutes we would stretch the limits of our collective talent and trust. Simple repositions were replaced with near-vertical whifferdills and barrel rolls around dazzling towers of clouds. Those watching from the ground could trace our every turn and roll, sketched with long, elegant contrails. The beauty of it all was matched only by the surge in energy around me.

As I repositioned the diamond for our pitch up to land, I looked one last time over my left shoulder, through Animal to the team below—and somehow I knew I was taking a mental picture for life. It was the still frame of our team at its absolute best.

The effects of drafting are as emotional as they are physically real, and they can accelerate much more than your team. It all begins with a dream so big it can be achieved only with the kind of growth and acceleration that come through collective effort. When you reach back into the chests of your people and pull them forward on their passions, their needs, and their desires, they will accelerate *you* in ways you can now imagine. And when that surge hits your wing, you'll take your own picture—a picture you will cherish for the rest of your days as the moment when you pulled the best out of your team, and they pulled the very best out of you.

Glossary

authority The power to give orders, make decisions, and direct or control someone or something.

biases Internal layers of protection that help us resist putting our physical, emotional, or financial well-being at risk.

closure Narrowing a gap between objects (planes, entities, or people) physically or psychologically.

commitment The demonstrated will to deliver for the people around you.

confidence One's faith in people—in their leadership, faculties, and judgment.

crosscheck Taking stock of your immediate environment by shifting your focus between two or more objects.

drafting *(aerodynamics)* The phenomenon whereby two objects moving close together sustain a faster speed than either object could achieve on its own. *(teamwork)* The phenomenon inspired by the aerodynamic property of bodies moving closely together; it requires leaders to inspire closure between individuals and entities to deliver cohesion, unity of effort, and team acceleration.

edge An attitude, a tone, an expectation of accountability that compels your team to act on your authority and follow your lead.

emotional hook An emotion that lives or is inspired to exist in an individual that is so powerful that it drives his or her behavior.

empowerment Granting your authority to a subordinate for the execution of a significant task, based on and framed by the expectations, resources, boundaries, and guidance you give.

engagement Your presence and one-on-one interactions with the people on your team.

friction Refining or challenging a thought, proposed course of action, or direction through a suggestion, statement, or question.

gap Physical or emotional distance caused by a lack of competence, a lack of confidence, or an unmet social need that degrades performance.

integrity How you add up. How your engagements with the pillars of faith, family, friends, health, and work measure up to the values you convey.

leadership principles Basic rules and beliefs that guide a leader's actions.

loyalty Cohesion within a relationship—the kind that can be built only on the foundation of commitment. It is fostered by a leader's willingness to go the distance to support his or her team without the expectation that they will respond in kind.

onboarding program The program or process teams offer new hires to orient them to their new environment and to give them the technical and social footing they need to take their place on the team.

organizational principles The foundational beliefs that fuel a company's mission, values, and goals and its day-to-day behavior.

passions The foundational—the most important—elements in an individual's life that drive his or her actions. Passions are the behind-the-scenes motivators that make individuals' motors run.

personal principles Fundamental values that drive an individual's behavior and reasoning.

pillars of life Five major areas that individuals can develop in their lives to support their well-being and drive their actions: faith, family, friends, health, and work. Some people have all five pillars at work in their lives; others develop only one or two.

position An individual's persona, or public face; it can be expressed in different ways.

preference A subjective feeling of liking or wanting something more than another thing.

pride Feelings of deep pleasure or satisfaction that arise from your achievements or from those of someone or something close to you.

principle A moral rule or belief that helps you know right from wrong and that dictates or helps shape your decisions and actions.

respect A feeling of admiration or high regard for the qualities of another.

ritual A recurring event that brings the team together; it should be simple, sustainable, all-inclusive, and always elevating.

spin-up To bring new hires up to speed with the tempo and technical faculties required in their jobs.

traction The footing a leader offers new hires that allows them to take their place in, and feel the first effects of, the leader's draft.

trust The willingness to put yourself or your team at risk in the belief that another will follow through on a task, in a role, or with a mission.

Acknowledgments

would like to thank the following people.

My beautiful wife, Lil, and two incredible sons, Harrison and Walker, for their support and understanding as I spent most every waking moment of free time for months on end to complete this book.

My dad and mom—James and Joyce Venable—for their constant love and support.

My brother, James L. Venable Jr., for being the first to read my concept of drafting and who encouraged me to go forward in way that only a big brother can.

Bob Korzeniewski, one of the greatest leaders and friends I have had the great fortune to know.

The Shepherd—Rob Jolles—who is one of the most talented, selfless, and giving men I have ever had the pleasure of knowing. Without his encouragement and gentle prods, this book would have never seen the light of day.

Sarah Madden, my manuscript editor, who suffered through and corrected some of the worst grammar that has ever made it to a page.

Nancy Breuer, my developmental editor, whose deft hand did so much more than eliminate the million-odd metaphor train wrecks in my manuscript.

Neil Maillet at Berrett-Koehler, one of the finest
editors in world.

JR Reid, Colonel Pete Ahern (USMC, Retired),
Tom Gregg, Curt "Jar" Sheldon, Subodh Nayar, and John
Satyshur for their willingness to review and refine the
manuscript from its earliest stages.

The volunteers and members of Career Network
Ministry at McLain Bible Church, whose constant encouragement and enthusiasm kept a following wind at my back
through the highs and lows of this effort.

Al Burkes, Lieutenant General Tod "TD" Wolters
(USAF), Paul "Ack" Ackerman, Dave "Bounce" Burnett,
Steve "Boz" Bozarth, Joe Shirey, and the other extraordinary
friends and leaders in and out of the Air Force who influenced me along life's path.

Finally, I would like to thank the incredible team of
Thunderbirds I had the pleasure of serving with for two
awe-inspiring years. Your professionalism, dedication,
and constant drive for excellence keep me striving to be
a better man.

Index

About the Author

JV Venable is a graduate of the USAF's Fighter Weapons School (Top Gun) and has flown fighter aircraft all over the world. He has led individuals, teams, and organizations as large as 1,100 people at the highest ends of performance and risk in both peacetime and combat. Most notable was his time as the commander and demonstration leader of the USAF jet demonstration team, the Thunderbirds.

JV is an inspirational speaker, seminar leader, and coach on building and leading high-performance teams, and his deft candor and indelible integrity enhance the outcomes of every organization he touches.

He lives with his beautiful wife, Lil, and two sons, Harrison and Walker, in northern Virginia.

Berrett–Koehler
Publishers

Berrett-Koehler is an independent publisher dedicated to an ambitious mission: *connecting people and ideas to create a world that works for all.*

We believe that to truly create a better world, action is needed at all levels—individual, organizational, and societal. At the individual level, our publications help people align their lives with their values and with their aspirations for a better world. At the organizational level, our publications promote progressive leadership and management practices, socially responsible approaches to business, and humane and effective organizations. At the societal level, our publications advance social and economic justice, shared prosperity, sustainability, and new solutions to national and global issues.

A major theme of our publications is "Opening Up New Space." Berrett-Koehler titles challenge conventional thinking, introduce new ideas, and foster positive change. Their common quest is changing the underlying beliefs, mindsets, institutions, and structures that keep generating the same cycles of problems, no matter who our leaders are or what improvement programs we adopt.

We strive to practice what we preach—to operate our publishing company in line with the ideas in our books. At the core of our approach is stewardship, which we define as a deep sense of responsibility to administer the company for the benefit of all of our "stakeholder" groups: authors, customers, employees, investors, service providers, and the communities and environment around us.

We are grateful to the thousands of readers, authors, and other friends of the company who consider themselves to be part of the "BK Community." We hope that you, too, will join us in our mission.

A BK Business Book

This book is part of our BK Business series. BK Business titles pioneer new and progressive leadership and management practices in all types of public, private, and nonprofit organizations. They promote socially responsible approaches to business, innovative organizational change methods, and more humane and effective organizations.

Berrett–Koehler
Publishers

Connecting people and ideas
to create a world that works for all

Dear Reader,

Thank you for picking up this book and joining our worldwide community of Berrett-Koehler readers. We share ideas that bring positive change into people's lives, organizations, and society.

To welcome you, we'd like to offer you a free e-book. You can pick from among twelve of our bestselling books by entering the promotional code **BKP92E** here: http://www.bkconnection.com/welcome.

When you claim your free e-book, we'll also send you a copy of our e-newsletter, the *BK Communiqué*. Although you're free to unsubscribe, there are many benefits to sticking around. In every issue of our newsletter you'll find

• A free e-book
• Tips from famous authors
• Discounts on spotlight titles
• Hilarious insider publishing news
• A chance to win a prize for answering a riddle

Best of all, our readers tell us, "Your newsletter is the only one I actually read." So claim your gift today, and please stay in touch!

Sincerely,

Charlotte Ashlock
Steward of the BK Website

Questions? Comments? Contact me at bkcommunity@bkpub.com.

Certified

Corporation
bcorporation.net